Martha
and

Mary Ola

MY DAUGHTER, MY TEACHER:

Mary Ann, Autistic in English and Spanish

Martha Hanes Ziegler

iUniverse, Inc.
New York   Bloomington

My Daughter, My Teacher: Mary Ann, Autistic in English and Spanish

iUniverse books may be ordered through booksellers or by contacting:

iUniverse
1663 Liberty Drive
Bloomington, IN 47403
www.iuniverse.com
1-800-Authors (1-800-288-4677)

ISBN: 978-1-4502-2916-6 (pbk)
ISBN: 978-1-4502-2917-3 (ebk)

Printed in the United States of America

iUniverse rev. date: 5/04/2010

Dedicated to my other teacher, Mary Ann's brother Fred

Contents

Preface

"Yo soy allegre asser aqui." (I am happy to be here.)

My autistic daughter, Mary Ann, taught me that sentence the day before I left for San Juan, Puerto Rico, to help my friends and colleagues celebrate the twentieth anniversary of their parent center for children with disabilities. My pronunciation is almost unintelligible, but hers is perfect—at least as perfect as that of her teachers and the actors on the TV program, *Sesame Street*. Mary Ann is the only member of our family who speaks Spanish, and we all are proud of her accomplishment, even though she is autistic in Spanish as well as English. Her favorite Spanish words include *daysiuno* (breakfast), *carne* (meat), and other words that refer to food that she knows but I don't. Her English vocabulary is similarly loaded with words about food, including "scalloped oysters," "Peking duck," "pesto," and "lobster bisque."

With the steadily increasing numbers of children diagnosed, or at least labeled, with some form of autism, I feel compelled to share my daughter's story of hope, her amazing accomplishments, and her continuing progress throughout her adult years.

Mary Ann was diagnosed in the spring of 1966, at a time when autism was so rare that most of us, including physicians, had never even heard the term. It still is not clear whether the rarity was actual, simply a fact of misdiagnosis much of the time, of a strange mixture of labels, of no one keeping count, or a combination of these factors.

A January 2009 article in *Scientific American* describes a new study by researchers at the University of California. This study reports a sevenfold increase in autism in California over the last fifteen years and a similar dramatic increase throughout the nation. The article maintains that this increase cannot be explained simply by changes in diagnosis and that, "The scientists who authored the new study advocate a nationwide shift in autism research to focus on potential factors in the environment that babies and fetuses are exposed to, including pesticides, viruses, and chemicals in household products."[1]

Fortunately, recent years have seen a huge increase in research on nearly all aspects of autism: possible causes; more precise description of the symptoms, especially sensory and movement abnormalities; treatment and educational methods; and family support. As Mary Ann's experience indicates, children on the autism spectrum can benefit greatly from learning alongside their non-disabled peers. Furthermore, their inclusion in "regular classes" increases their acceptance as real people with individual desires and talents, even into their adult lives. They are much less likely to be feared and shunned, and more likely to be treated with interest, curiosity, and respect.

In recent decades, adult self-advocates like Temple Grandin, Donna Williams, Bill Stillman, Alex Michaels, Sue Rubin, Stephen Shore, and others have been immensely helpful in teaching us the firsthand experience of living on the autism spectrum. In addition, they continue to hammer home the importance of thinking "from the inside out" and "presuming intellect."

These admonitions mean that we must learn to look at life from the point of view of the person on the autism spectrum, including that person's interests, talents, experience, and individual needs. In other words, we should stop concentrating on the old "fixing the broken doll" approach, the apt description voiced by Ann Turnbull, co-founder of the Beach Center on Disability at the University of Kansas.

High on the list of remaining unmet needs is the whole area of adult living, with questions of independence, self-advocacy, continuing education, appropriate employment, and optimal living arrangements. As parents we must occasionally accept unwelcome compromises and disappointments. For instance, Mary Ann has often lost a meaningful job through no fault of her own—the relocation of a mortgage company where she did computer input work, the closing of a bakery, and a decision by a meat-packing plant to outsource their laundry. She happens to have a nearly ideal living situation, close to the center of the

---

1   http://www.scientificamerican.com/article.cfm?id=autism-rise-driven-by-environment

town where she grew up, but that outcome was the result of hard work by me and a group of friends plus a big piece of luck.

It may be helpful to remind ourselves that our other, non-disabled children may not quite achieve our ideal goals either. They may not go to Harvard, and they may never live in a mansion overlooking the ocean, but we do our best. What we really want for all our children, with or without disabilities, is a happy, productive life that includes friends, continued learning and growing, and opportunities to participate in and contribute to their community.

We often forget that many of the challenges faced by adults with autism or any disability are actually difficulties inadvertently built into our overall community structures. For instance, for those outside a large city, public transportation is essentially nonexistent—we are a car-driving nation, and not just car-driving but individually car-driving. It is not possible or desirable for all adults with disabilities, or all senior citizens, to live in large cities. As a young adult, Mary Ann had to give up attending a community college and working at a job in downtown Boston because of impossible transportation barriers, although eventually some situations did improve.

Mary Ann is not simply a living, walking label. She is a lovely, often charming, musically talented woman with a sense of humor who sometimes engages in annoying repetitive behavior. More than many "typical" women her age, she is always eager to improve both her behavior and her language.

As Mary Ann's mother, I present her story in order to share some of the possibilities and, yes, the joys of a life that started with mystery and frustration. Because of Mary Ann I have learned much directly from her, also from many of the professionals who have served her, from reading and attending conferences and workshops, and finally, from the many parents throughout the country with whom I have been privileged to work.

Therefore I present this story from the experience of motherhood and advocacy, not as a professional in autism or special education. I hope, though, that professionals will learn from Mary Ann's story and I hope families will gain new insight and hope from our family's experience.

Note: Several chapters end with what I have termed a "Food Note," an irresistible pun and a regular reminder of Mary Ann's overriding interest in food.

Mary Ann in the kitchen at her adult residence

Background

Whenas in silks my Julia goes,
Then, then, methinks, how sweetly flows
The liquefaction of her clothes!

Next, when I cast mine eyes and see
That brave vibration each way free,
—O how that glittering taketh me!

"Upon Julia's Clothes," by Robert Herrick

In the early 1950s, I was totally absorbed with seventeenth century lyric poetry, particularly the Cavalier poets and especially Robert Herrick. An Anglican minister, Herrick lived for eighty-three years, from the time of Shakespeare and Ben Jonson, through the time of John Donne and the other metaphysical poets, and right through the time of John Milton. Herrick never married, so far as we know, but nevertheless his poetry expressed immense sensuality and appreciation of beautiful young women. As with so many of the Renaissance poets, including Shakespeare, the biographical information about Herrick is very thin.

As a graduate student in English literature, preparing to teach in college, I was enthralled with all this beautiful language. As a student at the University of Rochester, I wrote my master's thesis on Herrick's poetry and continued to concentrate on his work as I studied for a doctorate at Indiana University.

During these years, I was consumed with the delights of learning and thoughts about a future filled with the pleasures of teaching. Marriage and family were way down on my priority list. Looking back, I must admit that I was consumed with my own selfish pleasures: enjoying a summer course with Leslie Fiedler, a famous writer on Mark Twain, and spending an evening drinking beer with Leon Edel, the author of the definitive study of Henry James.

Meanwhile, I was developing a relationship with George Ziegler, an optical scientist whom I had met in Rochester. I have often joked that George and I met when we lived together. We each rented a room in the home of University of Rochester history professor, Arthur J. May and his wife. George designed sophisticated optical systems at Bausch and Lomb well before that company hit the jackpot with contact lenses. Among many complex optical systems, George helped develop the lens system for the first Xerox copier and he designed the periscope for the first nuclear submarine. He held eleven patents.

As I worked on my master's thesis, George helped me translate the only definitive book on Robert Herrick, which happened to be written in French. George's mastery of French was better than mine and he also was fluent in German. George and I were just beginning to know each other when the time came for me to continue my education. It was largely accidental that I went to Indiana University in Bloomington. The teaching fellowship I was offered meant that I could afford to continue my studies.

George came to visit my family in Fort Wayne, Indiana, and I visited his family in Greencastle, Pennsylvania. We all became closer over time, even writing frequent letters the old fashioned way, with pen and paper. After two years of a long-distance relationship, we became engaged and we married in the summer of 1955, before I would have completed my PhD. In those days, the husband's work came first, the wife's second if at all, and thus we had to live close to the Rochester location of Bausch and Lomb.

I was fortunate in being able to find a position as substitute English professor for three successive full-time professors when they took sabbatical leaves at the State University of New York at Brockport, just twenty miles west of Rochester. For the three years, George and I lived in Brockport, and he commuted to work by car and I walked to work. After three years, there were no more sabbatical vacancies for me and no new openings; we then moved to Rochester. Again, I was lucky in finding a position as public relations director at the Health Association of Rochester and Monroe County—a job that lasted a year or so.

My first responsibility in this new job was conducting the annual Christmas Seal drive—for many years the major fundraising effort of the Tuberculosis Society of America (now American Lung Association). With absolutely no experience, I hardly knew where to begin. I was saved by a baseball player, Red Schoendienst, legendary second baseman for the St. Louis Cardinals and later manager of the team. He famously battled tuberculosis during the Christmas Seal campaign and I was able to exploit his illness, including an editorial I wrote for the *Rochester Democrat and Chronicle*. Schoendienst's illness was especially important because it struck a major blow against the myth that TB only occurred in poor, unhealthy people.

After two years living in Rochester, George and I decided to buy a house and start planning a family. Finally, at age thirty, I learned to drive. Meanwhile, I became active in Women Strike for Peace, a political action group working to end atmospheric testing of atomic weapons. WSP was founded by Dagmar Wilson, a children's book illustrator, involved Bella Abzug, a lawyer who later became a member of Congress, and Alva Helen Pauling, wife of Nobel winner Linus Pauling. That work was a major help in preparing me for later advocacy and organizing in my disability work. I even learned my way around Washington DC during an early, big demonstration and later during the Cuban Missile Crisis.

Women Strike for Peace and its partner organizations did, in fact, succeed in persuading Congress to end the atmospheric testing of nuclear weapons. Many years later, I wondered if the prevalence of strontium 90 in the atmosphere and in the ground may have contributed to our daughter's disability. George's military service at the end of World War II raised similar flags. He served in Japan soon after the armistice and he actually took several trips to Hiroshima shortly after the bombing.

Once my pregnancy was confirmed in the spring of 1963, I started reading Dr. Benjamin Spock's book, *Baby and Child Care,* and also *Studies in Child Development,* by Arnold Gesell. I had no direct experience with infants and young children because my mother, sister, and other relatives lived four hundred miles away in Indiana, and when I was teaching at Brockport I was the youngest person on the faculty. That last fact meant that all of my professional friends had had their children several years earlier.

On December 29, 1963, shortly after midnight, George drove

me through the snow from our home in Gates, a suburb just west of Rochester, to Strong Memorial Hospital, where Mary Ann arrived a few hours later. She was born breech, a fact that meant little to me at the time because I knew so little about such things.

Mary Ann arrived a few years before the renewed interest in breastfeeding had taken hold. I had learned a little about the importance of breastfeeding, but I was amazed by the very negative response of nurses at the hospital—they clearly thought that I was way too demanding because I wanted some information and assistance. Despite my concentrated efforts and help from friends in La Leche League, Mary Ann was never able to nurse. The breech birth had caused some damage on one side of her mouth, and I assumed that this was the reason for her difficulty.

The last thing that entered my mind was the possibility that my dear daughter, Mary Ann, would spend a lifetime serving as my teacher and also as teacher to many others. Here was a role reversal I could never have anticipated—my formal education had prepared me to teach English in college, not to teach children with disabilities or even to study linguistics or behavioral psychology. As I look back at my years of immersion in seventeenth century English poetry, I am struck by the irony of living with a lovely daughter whose very life is one continuous poem, filled with music, color, and metaphor.

Martha and Mary Ann (age one)

PART I:

From Shock to Celebration

CHAPTER 1

Early Months and Years: What Is This Thing Called Autism?

Mary Ann on her second birthday

On a fine spring day in 1966, I drove in a state of shock along Route 6 and then down Route 7 in Connecticut from the Southbury Training School back home to Norwalk, with my beautiful, quiet little daughter in the car seat next to me.

"What is autism? What does it mean?" I kept asking myself. And then "What should we do? What have we done that caused this?" What did the doctor mean when he motioned up the hill behind him and said, "There are probably four hundred people like her up here"?

In April 1966, our family had moved from Rochester to Norwalk, Connecticut. Mary Ann was not quite two and a half, and her brother Fred was seven months old. Luckily, Fred was conceived before we knew anything about Mary Ann's disability. When the first child is diagnosed with autism, regardless of its form or severity, it still is not easy for parents to decide to have more children.

George had decided to leave Bausch and Lomb to advance his career. This turned out to be the first of many moves, each depending on federal defense contracts. Incredibly, each move gave us more information about autism and what to do and not do for Mary Ann.

In Norwalk, we encountered two pediatricians who had some familiarity with autism, and one of them immediately referred Mary Ann to Dr. Herman Yannet at Southbury Training School. We soon realized that this early recognition of Mary Ann's autism was very, very unusual at that time and for many years afterward as well. We later learned that often children with autism were first diagnosed as hearing impaired because of their lack of spoken language and apparent avoidance of social contact. Many were considered mentally ill or simply mentally retarded; the term "childhood schizophrenia" was commonly applied to them.

As I look back over these forty-three years, it occurs to me that it may have been a good thing that we were so totally ignorant about autism. We had no immediate cure-all offers to study and withstand, no psychoanalysis of George and me, no blaming us as cold or inadequate parents, no megavitamin therapy, no "aversive therapy," no controversy about vaccinations—we just had to love and help our dear daughter. As the years went by we did, of course, learn a lot, primarily from Mary Ann herself, with help from a few forward-thinking experts.

Today, we know that autism is a neurological disorder that interferes with language and social interaction. Diagnosis still requires observation of behavior—no blood test or X-ray can give a quick answer. Recently, Margaret Bauman and other physicians have discovered underlying gastrointestinal disorders.[2] These can cause the strange behavior that

---

2   Dr. Margaret Bauman, pediatric neurologist at Harvard University, is a pioneer

basically results from pain—the child with autism lacks the language adequate to communicate the pain. Addressing the gastrointestinal pain reduces what had appeared to be antisocial behavior but was, in reality, an effort to communicate the pain and frustration.

In spite of some claims, there is no sure cure, although good teaching, therapy, love, and respect for the child as an individual person can often produce amazing progress. We know that the disorder varies greatly from one autistic person to another, sometimes appearing in the mild form called Asperger syndrome.

George and I feared that Mary Ann might never speak at all, much less learn a second language someday. Later that year, she underwent a comprehensive assessment at the Yale Child Study Center with Dr. Sally Provence, and it became clear that she exhibited nearly all the symptoms of severe, classical "Kanner" autism, not the milder variety now often called Asperger syndrome.[3] For instance, each time we visited Dr. Provence's office, Mary Ann immediately approached a metal crib that stood in one corner and she ran her fingers along the metal rails. We assume the sound and feel of this action must have calmed her to some extent. At this point, she was not speaking at all, not even able to answer questions.

At the Yale Child Study Center, Mary Ann underwent a thorough pediatric examination and also a thorough assessment by Dr. Peter Huttenlocher, a pediatric neurologist. In addition to autism, these specialists reported that Mary Ann probably had neurofibromatosis but they could not be certain.[4] From birth, Mary Ann's trunk displayed a pattern of brown spots, which meant nothing to me at the time, but I

---

in research identifying neuro-anatomical abnormalities in the limbic system and cerebellum of people with autism. In addition to several research consortiums, Dr. Bauman also founded LADDERS, a comprehensive diagnostic and therapeutic protocol for those on the autism spectrum.

3   Dr. Sally Provence, pediatrician and director of the Child Development Unit, Child Study Center, Yale University, died in 1993. She was a pioneer in child development both as a teacher and as a researcher.

4   Neurofibromatosis (NF) is a genetic disorder of the nervous system that primarily affects the development and growth of neural cell tissues. The disorder can cause tumors to grow on nerves and produce other abnormalities such as skin changes and bone deformities. Mary Ann has NF 1, the milder form; hers was apparently caused by a mutation, not by heredity. Autism often coincides with NF.

later learned that these spots are a primary symptom of NF. It was many years later, when Mary Ann was a young adult, that she experienced her one grand mal seizure and then, after thorough testing, was diagnosed with NF with certainty.

Like most parents in this situation, George and I wracked our brains trying to figure out what on earth had caused this disaster. What had we done wrong? Was there inheritance somewhere that we did not know about? By then, we had five nephews and a niece, all perfectly healthy. As I indicated earlier, George had served in the army in the final months of World War II. Could his two trips to Hiroshima shortly after the bombing in 1945 have caused a mutation? The science of genetics was still so primitive that there was no way of making any certain connection. However, more recent research indicates that George's untimely trips to Hiroshima were indeed a possible cause of Mary Ann's disability, though not a certainty, and they may also have contributed to George's fatal cancer forty-three years after his service in Japan.

As I indicated earlier, I think it was a good thing that our family was totally ignorant about autism. For instance, when George and I asked Dr. Provence to recommend books to read, she wisely advised that not much was available, and that it would be better to work with Mary Ann to help her. Luckily, we were too busy to go to the library and, of course, at that time there was no Internet. If we had found anything it would have been Bruno Bettelheim's new book insisting that the "refrigerator mother" was the cause of autism[5] or Leo Kanner's original article defining autism.[6] Kanner also began with a negative view about parenting, although he gradually changed that view.

Eventually, I recalled an article in *Scientific American* magazine about the "electronic boy."[7] However, as I thought about that article, I could see absolutely no connection between that boy and the strange, baffling, but beautiful little girl we were living with.

---

5   Bruno Bettelheim, *The Empty Fortress: Infantile Autism and the Birth of the Self* (New York: The Free Press, 1967).

6   Leo Kanner, "Autistic disturbances of affective contact,". *Nerv Child* (1943) 2: 217–50. Leo Kanner founded the first academic child psychiatry department at Johns Hopkins University Hospital. Kanner is considered the original definer of autism.

7   "Joey: A 'mechanical boy.'" *Scientific American*, 1959.

We followed Dr. Provence's advice with help from her social worker assistant, Mrs. Kirschner. George and I used our imagination and time to find every possible game and toy for Mary Ann that we hoped would promote social interaction and language. As a stay-at-home mother, I had the time to search the aisles of Woolworth's dime store (at that time there were very few shopping malls, but every town still had a fairly large, comprehensive dime store in the middle of downtown). For instance, I bought brightly colored placemats shaped like animals to stimulate mealtime conversation. Even baby brother Fred pitched in to help, probably hoping for a responsive playmate. Permanently fixed in my memory are his words to his sister when he was just two years old: "Dat's wight, Maymay, 'ap-poh'!" as we discussed fruit at the breakfast table.

Looking back, I realize we were doing an amateur version of Stanley Greenspan's Floortime, the relationship-based intervention now used almost everywhere with very young children with autism.[8] There is no question that Sally Provence and Mrs. Kirschner were way ahead of their time.

I sometimes forget that we were rearing our young children in an age when most mothers stayed home, perhaps doing some volunteer work but usually not pursuing a paid career or working five days a week. This was a fortunate situation for Mary Ann and me because there still were very few services for children like her. Later, when both children were in school and after housing costs had skyrocketed, I did join other mothers in the job market.

George and I had decided our daughter with autism would be that one in a hundred or so who would learn to speak. As I look back, I realize that we did not think in terms of *communication*, only *talking*, as if these were synonymous. Meanwhile, she was doing none of the cooing and babbling that normally lead to speaking.

As I indicated earlier, I had been using Dr. Benjamin Spock's book, *Baby and Child Care,* and following a book on child development by Arnold Gesell. Until one and a half to two years, Mary Ann was always

---

8   Dr. Stanley Greenspan, Clinical Professor of Psychiatry and Pediatrics, The George Washington University Medical School, developed the program Floortime, later called DIR/Floortime, to serve young children with autism. Along with Serena Wieder, Greenspan has continually refined his relationship-based approach to autism.

barely within the normal range of development, although on the outer edge of normal. However, later, after her diagnosis, I remembered several instances that might have provided clues. My mother, who lived four hundred miles away in Indiana and worked fulltime at General Electric, had come to visit when Mary Ann was two months old. She later told me she had noticed that when she was changing Mary Ann's diaper, holding her upright, that she did not push her feet against the changing table as most babies do. One time, when Mary Ann was around a year old, I held her in my arms to look out the window at a dog walking up the street; instead of looking at the dog, she looked at reflections and the surface of the glass in the window.

My sister Lois came to visit when Mary Ann was around seven months old. Not knowing that Mary Ann had not yet sat up on her own, Lois sat her on the floor with her back against the sofa, where she sat as relaxed and happy as could be and, after that, sat up on her own. This kind of unexpected achievement occurred several times over the years, with eating and drinking, for instance. Friends or relatives who knew little about Mary Ann's disability, and did know more than I did about what to expect from children, would correctly assume she could do things that were a surprise to me. In other words, some of what looked like late development may in reality have been my own inexperience with babies—until Mary Ann's birth, I had spent no time at all around infants and young children and was totally ignorant.

Later, I also recalled that during regular visits to the pediatrician in Rochester, the doctor would bend down and extend her arms to Mary Ann in what I now know was the "anticipatory gesture." Mary Ann never responded to this invitation. Likewise, Mary Ann did not extend her arms hoping to be picked up. At the time I was too ignorant, or perhaps unwilling, to recognize a problem. I can see how this kind of atypical behavior in an infant or toddler could have led earlier psychologists and psychiatrists to conclude that autism was associated with "cold mothering"—they were, after all, observing what looked like dysfunctional social interaction. Only now are we beginning to understand the basic biological, neurological, and genetic ways in which autism interferes with normal development.

Mary Ann totally skipped the crawling stage—she began to walk around twenty-three months. Some of Mary Ann's strange motor development can be attributed to what Dr. Martha Denckla and others refer to as "hypotonia" in many children with autism.[9] On the Internet, I discovered that this condition, which varies greatly in severity, can cause difficulty with sucking—sure enough, Mary Ann had been unable to breast feed. Presumably, today's occupational therapists help with this challenge.

When Mary Ann was a toddler, the most painful times for me were those instances when she would fall or suffer a minor hurt and it was impossible for me to console her. She simply did not respond at all, as most babies do, to hugging, kissing, and gentle assurances. She simply would continue to cry piteously. The difference was dramatized one time when her three-year-old brother burned his finger by touching a hot brick in front of the fireplace. It happened that the children's Grandmother Ziegler phoned shortly after this accident. When she spoke to him on the phone, and gently but firmly assured him it would be all well by the next morning, he almost immediately stopped crying and went on to other things. Such interventions never worked for Mary Ann.

In recent years, discoveries have been announced concerning the unusually large head size of many children with autism, and also the head size of many of the fathers. Throughout Mary Ann's infancy, our pediatrician carefully measured her head, always noting the unusually large size, and each time George laughed about his own large head size, once commenting that he always had difficulty finding a cap or hat large enough when he served in the army. Researchers at the Center for Autism Research at Children's Hospital in San Diego have found a correlation between autism and a rapidly growing head size during the first year or so of infancy.[10] Eric Courchesne and his colleagues say the abnormal growth in head size is probably an indication of a too-rapid, jumbled growth of the brain. The connection with the father's head size, however, is still not clear. Is this an indicator of a genetic propensity simply waiting for an environmental trigger?

Theories about the poorly controlled growth of the infant brain in

---

9   Dr. Martha Denckla is Director of Developmental Cognitive Neurology, Kennedy Krieger Institute and Professor of Neurology, Pediatrics, and Psychiatry at the Johns Hopkins University School of Medicine. She has done pioneering research in autism.

10   Eric Courchesne, *et al, Journal of the American Medical Association* (July 16, 2003).

autistic children have been emerging during recent years. It occurs to me that this jumbled, disorganized growth of the brain may also account for some of the savant characteristics, as well as the more obvious difficulties of language and social behavior. Savant characteristics are unusual, narrow abilities not usually shared with other people. Dustin Hoffman's character in the movie *Rainman* could look at a box of matches spilled on the floor and quickly announce the number of matches, always accurately. At one point in the past, an autistic person was actually called an idiot savant.

From the time Mary Ann could pose questions to others, she has regularly asked, "When is your birthday? What year were you born?" Once she gets the answer, she quickly tells the respondent the day of the week that he or she was born. She will also do the same quick calculation for a date in the future, her birthday for instance, or a holiday. She is never wrong.

Mary Ann was our first-born child and I was thirty-three, my husband George thirty-eight, when she was born. In addition, all our extended family members, our parents and siblings with their children, lived far away. Most of our professional friends either had no children or had had them several years earlier. Thus, George and I approached parenthood with complete, unadulterated ignorance. There were probably advantages as well as disadvantages stemming from our inexperience.

During those early months and years, my primary experience as a mother was bafflement and vague worry, not the shock and grief experienced by many mothers of children with disabilities. As I have come to know hundreds of parents over the years, I have concluded that the emotional experiences of parents probably differ largely on the basis of the time they learned about the disability. I believe our experience of gradually increasing worry is fundamentally different from that of parents whose children are born with an immediately identifiable disability such as Down syndrome or spina bifida. Then, of course, within these two categories, people vary greatly in their reactions, sometimes depending on such variables as the manner and knowledge of doctors and the accompanying reactions of extended family members and friends.

Unlike many mothers, in spite of advice from Dr. Provence, I was originally reluctant to connect with other parents of children with autism. As I have later thought about this resistance, I think I was afraid to find out how bad, how discouraging autism could be. In the course of my work in disability advocacy, I have learned that the immediate response to the discovery of a child's disability can vary greatly from one family to another and it is a mistake to make any assumptions about this.

One of my favorite stories comes from Ed Feinberg, a leading early childhood specialist in Maryland. Ed reports that soon after he received his doctorate and credential and began to work with families, he visited a family living in poverty in Appalachia with a newborn infant with Down syndrome. Each week when he went to visit the couple, both greeted him warmly and cheerfully, but they were crying by the time he left the house. Finally, after the third visit, the father said to him, "Dr. Feinberg, it would really be better if you do not come back anymore. Every time you come, we feel sadder afterward." Ed now jokes about the fact that his formal training had interfered with his ability to accept the happy contentment of a young couple with their baby daughter in spite of her disability.

Ed Feinberg's experience dramatically illustrates the error we commit when we assume we understand another person's emotional reaction either to a child's disability or to the children themselves. George and I were in shock not because of our direct experience with Mary Ann, but because we had no understanding of the disability, what to expect, what we should do, how to plan, or what the future would or could bring.

All these recollections about events in Mary Ann's first twelve to eighteen months led me to conclude that autism could, and should, be identified much earlier than it usually is, even today. Unfortunately, with today's financial pressures for quick, short visits with a doctor, these opportunities go right on being overlooked. With early identification, as early as twelve months, sometimes even sooner, children with autism could be receiving comprehensive interventions that almost certainly would ameliorate many of the problems of their disability. And before long, our knowledge of genetic and environmental causation will enable us to intervene directly to promote healthy development of the infant brain and nervous system.

Dr. William Condon, who counseled Mary Ann for many years during her adolescence and early adult years, did pioneering work in the way autistic people process sound.[11] By filming them listening to sound and recording the time from sound to reaction, Dr. Condon demonstrated a time lag between sound stimulus and response in autistic people. He also found that the longer the time lag, the more severe the autism. He concluded that his discovery probably could be utilized to diagnose this basic aspect of autism just days after a baby's birth. So far as I know, no one has yet followed up on Condon's discovery and developed the necessary equipment for this kind of screening. Dr. David Tremain has established Interactional Synchrony Studies, Inc., to at least promote Condon's ideas.[12]

Today, a child like Mary Ann would be in a comprehensive early-intervention program, probably starting at eighteen months, possibly at twelve months, receiving physical and occupational therapy, speech and language training, and help in developing social skills. Luckily, our family was able to provide or find some of these pieces by following our instincts in addition to suggestions from our friends at the Yale Child Study Center. However, a quality early-intervention program like those available today could have made an enormous difference in Mary Ann's life.

Nancy Wiseman, a talented parent of an autistic child, has developed a checklist that pediatricians and parents can use to foster the earliest possible identification of autism in young children.[13] She spearheaded a statewide campaign in New Jersey and later in Pennsylvania. Many professionals have recently jumped on board this effort. Early identification and early teaching and therapy certainly are important and I have always commended Nancy's work. However, I also urge some caution around recent extreme claims about early identification. Some of the more excessive statements say outright, or appear to imply, that treatment must occur "early or never"—a very unfair insinuation. Like everyone else, autistic children and adults continue to learn and grow, regardless of their beginnings. Mary Ann and some of our friends are prime examples. Good teaching and quality therapy—speech, music, physical and occupational therapy—can produce good results at any age.

---

11 Dr. Condon was retired as professor of psychology at Boston University.

12 See www.isautism.com.

13 See Appendix A.

Wiseman calls her program "First Signs," and it works as an effort to help parents and physicians more readily identify the earliest signs of autism or other developmental delays. With the help of leading professionals in autism, Wiseman has developed two checklists. The longer one, called "Hallmark Developmental Milestones," is based on two-, three-, and twelve-month intervals.

Following is Wiseman's shorter checklist, called "Red Flags," developed primarily for parents.

The following red flags may indicate a child is at risk for atypical development and is in need of an immediate evaluation. If your baby shows any of these signs, please ask your pediatrician or family practitioner for an immediate evaluation:

- No big smiles or other warm, joyful expressions by six months or thereafter
- No back-and-forth sharing of sounds, smiles, or other facial expressions by nine months or thereafter
- No babbling by twelve months
- No back-and-forth gestures, such as pointing, showing, reaching, or waving by twelve months
- No words by sixteen months
- No two-word meaningful phrases (without imitating or repeating) by twenty-four months
- Any loss of speech or babbling or social skills at any age[14]

In reviewing this list, I can see that Mary Ann met every one of the indicators, except the last one, which applies only to those children who undergo sudden regression after several months of normal development. As an inexperienced new mother, I was not aware of Mary Ann's missing steps during the first six months or so. However, I remember being surprised when my friend, June Burke, held Mary Ann in her lap and elicited a smile from her after some effort. I had not realized I should try a little harder.

---

14   "Red Flags" was compiled from the following sources: S.I. Greenspan, *Building Healthy Minds*, (New York, NY: Perseus Books, 1999).; P.A. Filipek, et al., "Practice parameter: Screening and Diagnosis of autism." *Neurology* (2000), 55: 468–79.

Even without a diagnosis, George and I were unwittingly utilizing our own version of some aspects of Floortime, Son-Rise, and other child-centered approaches that later were developed and refined by knowledgeable professionals. We read to her, always letting her choose the book, and we did everything we could to engage her in play, for example playing peekaboo and other baby games. However, she did not respond as she should have.

CHAPTER 2

"He Have Brown Hands." Emerging Language and Primitive Beginnings of Education

Mary Ann, age four, at home in Norwalk, Connecticut

Around age three, Mary Ann began to repeat single words—repeating only nouns and only after her brother Fred said them first, never after me or anyone else—as we looked at picture books together. Finally, one month before her fourth birthday, Mary Ann uttered her first spontaneous words: "kitty cat!" We had gone to the Fairfield, Connecticut, home of a self-appointed "cat rescue" lady to acquire a pet cat. When the woman brought the first candidate up from the basement, Mary Ann said her three-syllable phrase with great excitement and delight. George and I were stunned. She had occasionally repeated single nouns after her brother Fred, but she had never on her own initiated any speech.

Our family loved Connecticut. We enjoyed our many new friends who had come from various parts of the country, many commuting to exciting jobs in New York City, and we treasured our proximity to the shore of the Long Island Sound. Gradually, George and my new friends helped me overcome my Midwestern qualms and learn to prepare and enjoy flounder, swordfish, and lobster.

We especially enjoyed Sherwood Island State Park, where we would take the two children on crisp weekend afternoons in the fall, after everyone else had deserted the beach. On those lovely autumn days we were spared worries about interference from other children and questions or pressures from other adults. While George played with Fred, I would have to keep one hand on Mary Ann—if I let go, she would start walking, in a straight line, ignoring everything in her path, until I could reach her and grab her. It was fruitless to yell "Stop!" One day, when I took her to a neighbor's house where there was a small pond in the back yard, she walked straight into the pond, ignoring the water. I had to go straight in behind her—dress, shoes and all—to pull her out or she surely would have drowned. In spite of this near disaster, she has never learned to fear the water. A few years later, she learned to swim and became a superb swimmer, often swimming laps when she had the opportunity. To this day, when we are traveling, she always demands a motel or hotel with a pool.

George was very proud of his new Volvo. One Sunday afternoon he took us all for a ride through the gentle hills of nearby New Canaan, Connecticut. Unfortunately, Mary Ann was still very unhappy with car riding; she christened the new car as only a sick child can do. Until about age four, Mary Ann hated to go anywhere in the car. We avoided taking her as much as possible, but sometimes we had no choice, for example to shop for shoes. She would begin to cry as soon as we went out the front door and never stop until we returned, through that same front door. Today's occupational therapists, experts in sensory problems, and especially those of autistic people, could probably explain this discomfort in a minute and recommend effective therapy. All I know is that around age four, it cleared up.

During these early years, I often felt that we were in the process of creating a person. I am not so arrogant that I literally thought this, but that is what it often felt like. Unlike the more familiar hyperactive child with autism who is often wrongly viewed as aggressive, Mary Ann was withdrawn. George and I (and often little brother Fred) worked to teach her to feed herself, to climb the stairs, to talk, to interact, to play, and to participate in life.

For one year, from ages three and a half to four and a half, on the recommendation of Dr. Provence and others at Yale, Mary Ann attended a half-day "regular" preschool in neighboring Rowayton, Connecticut. Unfortunately, the teacher, who had experience with autistic children, became seriously ill and had to leave in the middle of the year. Mary Ann did not really participate—she would play only alongside, but never with, the other children, and she cried a lot.

In the spring of 1968, I called the superintendent of schools in Norwalk, Connecticut, to inquire about a school program for Mary Ann for the following year. He replied "We are thinking about starting classes for retarded children next year; we have not thought about autistic children yet." Implicit in that response was the lack of any requirement that the local public schools had to educate my daughter; this was strictly a family challenge. It was still legal for the public schools to totally exclude children like Mary Ann, even after they reached so-called "mandatory" school age.

A few months later George changed jobs and we found ourselves moving again—this time to Huntington, Long Island, New York. Mary Ann was four and a half, and her brother Fred was not quite three. Once settled on Long Island, we found Eva Frendzel, an incredibly skilled speech and language therapist who was way ahead of her time. She came to our house for an hour once a week, bringing along puzzles, games, and a large coffee can full of toy animals of various sizes. While Mary Ann worked with "Miss Eva" I did not exist, even though I usually sat watching, listening, and learning, about six feet away from the two of them. I remember vividly the first time Mary Ann looked up at me, indicating awareness of my presence during one of these sessions—it was as if her sphere of awareness had suddenly expanded by several feet.

When we moved to Huntington, I did not even knock on the schoolhouse door—by then I knew how useless it would be. In our three years on Long Island, Mary Ann attended three different private programs. The first one was a "psychotherapeutic" preschool that was clearly useless, even to someone as uninformed as I was. Nothing productive occurred in that two-hour program. So far as I could see, there was no activity, no learning, going on. One boy was always huddled in a fetal position high in one corner of the room, atop a stack of pillows on a chair.

After about six weeks of little Fred and me driving Mary Ann many miles into the next county for this worthless program, I found another, much better preschool. This was a federally-funded preschool for autistic children—pretty good for the time. (Later, after I had learned more, I realized this preschool was probably based on Montessori principles.) And I only had to drive her to a central pickup point, a couple of miles away, where a special, publicly-funded bus took her to the preschool.

After Mary Ann outgrew the preschool program, I enrolled her in a private, special day school for autistic children, the Suffolk Center for Emotionally Disturbed Children (now called the Developmental Disabilities Institute), patterned after the League School in Brooklyn. The League School was one of the first schools in the nation designed specifically for autistic children. Overall, the Suffolk Center was a good program, headed by a knowledgeable director who had up-to-the-minute training, but it too was twenty some miles away, on the opposite shore of the island in the town of Bay Shore. At this point, the State of New York paid for transportation along with a small monthly stipend toward tuition. However, for each of these school programs, our family paid a large portion of the tuition costs and, of course, did fundraising to help keep the school afloat.

Until the early 1970s, local public schools in most states had absolutely no obligation to educate children like Mary Ann. If they did anything at all, regardless of quality or appropriateness, it was a favor that parents should have been grateful for.

As Mary Ann worked on puzzles with Miss Eva, it became clear that she put them together based only on the shape of the pieces, not on the pictures themselves. One way to describe this experience is to say the pictures contained no gestalt for her. Looking back, I have to wonder if much of her life was like that—no gestalt most of the time.

This is just another way of trying to understand what goes on in the mind and life of a child whose abilities and perceptions are scattered all over the map, with no clear integration. Children like Mary Ann are prime living examples of Howard Gardner's theory of multiple intelligences, though perhaps extreme examples.[15] Furthermore, people with autism have extra trouble integrating these varying abilities. Mary Ann and other children like her are such heroes as they try valiantly to make sense of what must be a chaotic world.

In her early years she was very fond of interesting textures. On the first cold Saturday in the fall of 1968, I took her grocery shopping with me at King Kullen, a large supermarket in Huntington. It seemed to me that everyone in the store was wearing either a corduroy or suede jacket that day; Mary Ann stroked each one, clearly enjoying the special feel of these fabrics. The customers, especially the women, would say, "Oh, it's all right, I don't mind." However, when we got to the checkout counter, I looked up and noticed a young man in the next line over, wearing corduroy pants and a sheepish, dazed look on his face. I could not help wondering if Mary Ann had gently stroked his corduroy pants.

Throughout her life, Mary Ann has disliked plain white bread. She would remove the hamburger from the bun, eat the meat, and leave the bun. If somehow forced to eat the bread she would gag on it. I always assumed this was another bizarre aspect of her autism, until recently when I was visiting my sister in Indiana. I happened to mention this characteristic to her, and she replied, "Oh, don't you remember? I always hated plain white bread too. I'm just like Mary Ann —I almost gag on it too." Mary Ann's autism prevents her from discreetly hiding this strong personal preference or joking about it as her aunt does.

Here again, we see the complex interplay of sensory challenges and difficulty with communication. Frequently with an autistic child, it is difficult to break through the language barrier to find the true problem the child is facing. I have often commented that being a parent of an autistic child requires detective skills.

Around age six, Mary Ann became fascinated with hair. She

---

15   Howard Gardner is Hobbs Professor of Cognition and Education, at the Harvard Graduate School of Education. Gardner's original seven intelligences are linguistic, logical-mathematical, musical, bodily-kinesthetic, spatial, interpersonal, and intrapersonal. *Frames of Mind: The Theory of Multiple Intelligences*, Basic Books, 10th edition, 1993.

especially loved long hair and Afros. Whenever she met a new woman, she would stroke the woman's hair, with or without permission of course. When I took her shopping for clothes (a chore that she hated), she would approach each mannequin in turn and stroke the hair. This happened to be a period when most women were wearing long hair, which was especially attractive to Mary Ann. Luckily she never pulled hair, just stroked it gently, clearly enjoying the tactile sensation.

Mary Ann never played with toys in an "appropriate" way. She would grab a doll by the ankles and then shake it up and down. In fact, Mary Ann probably has never perceived a doll as a small or imitation person, only as a plastic object that could just as well be a wooden block. Just recently, she and I were at a friend's house and she spotted a Barbie doll with long blonde hair. She grabbed the doll and shook the hair back and forth, not even looking at it as a doll. Recent neurological research about mirror neurons may explain this strange behavior.[16]

The research shows that the mirror neurons in people with autism respond only to what the autistic person is doing and not to what other people are doing. In most people, these mirror neurons respond both to the "doer" and also to other people. Some researchers call these the "monkey-see, monkey-do" cells. In other words, the monkey's mirror neurons fire both when the monkey performs a particular action and also when the monkey observes another monkey, or person, perform the same action. However, the autistic person's mirror neurons do not function in the second instance.

Throughout Mary Ann's school years, we were excited as she continued to learn and make progress slowly but surely. Then suddenly she would appear to stop moving ahead, reaching a plateau and staying there for several weeks or months. Each time, just as we were losing all hope for more progress, especially with language, she would suddenly leap forward again and then continue to progress. I often felt as though she needed to pause occasionally to internalize, or integrate, what she

---

16   Mirella Dapretto, "Understanding emotions in others: mirror neuron dysfunction in children with autism spectrum disorders," *Nature Neuroscience*, Vol. 9, No. 1, 28–30, 2006–01. New imaging research at UCLA shows that children with autism have virtually no activity in a key part of the brain's mirror neuron system while imitating and observing emotions. See also *Scientific American* (November 2006).

had been learning. Also, it may well be that most children learn in this manner but that they have shorter, less visible plateaus.

When we moved to Long Island and it was no longer easy to call Dr. Provence and her staff, I had to overcome my dread and get acquainted with other parents of autistic children. Of course several families, especially Carol and Dennis Hansen, were very helpful. During the previous couple of years they had worked together with other Long Island parents to found the Metropolitan New York chapter, and also the national, Autism Society. Years later I came to appreciate the major undertaking—the great efforts and sacrifices that these friends had expended in order to establish what has become the basic gathering place for families and professionals who are trying to learn and work for a better life for children and adults with autism. Like most organizations, Autism Society of America (ASA) has gone through one challenge after another, especially as controversial treatment approaches have appeared, one after another. However, the true miracle is the fact that the organization has continued to grow and thrive and to survive each crucial test. Today, parents can choose to connect with several other national organizations devoted to autism in addition to ASA. Some specialize in research (Autism Speaks, Cure Autism Now and National Alliance for Autism Research) and some in advocacy (Autism National Committee); many others exist at state and even local levels.

At one point I had an opportunity to hear a talk by Dr. Allan Cott, a pioneer in orthomolecular, or megavitamin, therapy. One of Dr. Cott's interests at the time was the application of this therapy as a treatment for autism. I was not persuaded that this would be useful for Mary Ann, but I did learn something important from his talk. Dr. Cott described some of the unusual sensory experiences of autistic children. He commented that when an autistic child stands at the top of a stairway and looks down, it may appear to that child that the stairs go on forever. That made sense. After Mary Ann started walking and had learned to climb up the stairs, she refused to come down the stairs on her own. She would stand or sit at the top and cry. I have long felt that Dr. Cott was probably correct in his interpretation; his observation was a precursor to some of the current findings by occupational therapists.

During these years, when Mary Ann was five and six, she became aware of skin color. Living in the suburbs in Connecticut, then Long

Island, and finally Lexington, Massachusetts, she rarely saw anyone other than Caucasian people, just like her and her family. Once in a while she would encounter an African American—one selling magazines door-to-door in Huntington, and occasionally one in the supermarket there. Always she would say with amazement, "He have brown hands!" Once, in the supermarket, an African American man was shopping two aisles away when Mary Ann said loudly, "He have brown hands!" Luckily, each time the person was most gracious, often quite touched by her obvious innocence.

During this period we also noticed some of her obsessions. One was her love of meat. When she was six, her speech therapist, Miss Eva, invited her to come to Yeshiva University in New York City where Miss Eva conducted a demonstration class for students studying speech and language therapy. After the class we went to lunch in a nice New York restaurant. We all ordered steak. Mary Ann ate all of hers and half of Miss Eva's.

In these early years, Mary Ann was obsessed with a single toy—first was a stuffed pony. Of course many children without disabilities insist on their "blankie" or other security item, but when her favorite toy was unavailable she was inconsolable. When one would wear out, I would rush to the store to buy an exact replacement. For three years, ages four to seven approximately, Mary Ann was obsessed with a gingerbread boy, a stuffed toy made by the Knickerbocker Company, the makers of Raggedy Ann and Andy. After about three replacements, disaster struck—suddenly no more gingerbread boys were available in the stores. When I called the Knickerbocker Company in New Jersey, the person who answered the phone greeted me with great suspicion and no information. Evidently she thought I wanted to make a copy to sell. I was desperate. Finally, I went to a fabric store in Huntington and bought material to make "new skin" for Gooey, the worn-out gingerbread boy. Mary Ann played with it, but it was never quite the same. Maybe I and the Knickerbocker Company had accidentally transitioned her away from this obsession.

On Long Island, a young clinical psychologist was a big help to me in locating programs for Mary Ann. Like practically all therapists at the time, he was not equipped to provide Mary Ann with any actual therapy, but he was great with referrals. I vividly remember one early trip to his office. In the waiting room, one chair in a corner contained a large stack of magazines. Mary Ann had to flip through every single page of every magazine, exhibiting one more of her obsessions. She did not really examine each page or so far as I could tell she did not count the pages—she simply seemed to be compelled to turn each page quickly. She still tends to do this with a new book or magazine. She must find some physical pleasure in the feel of folding a corner and turning the page.

On one visit, when Mary Ann was six, I proudly told the psychologist that she had kissed me. "Not on the mouth I hope!" he quickly responded. She had not kissed me on the mouth, but his response seemed to me so weird that after that, we always kissed on the mouth deliberately. By then I realized that kissing at all was very unusual for an autistic child. I still do not know why this psychologist was so adamant about this.

As Mary Ann slowly acquired more language, much of it was echolalic (verbatim repetition of something she had heard) and she continued to reverse the pronouns "you" and "I." To this day she will answer many questions, such as "Are you all right?" with the whole sentence, "Yes, I am," rather than simply "yes" or "um hm." Her friends with autism, including David Alterson, do the same thing. Furthermore, Mary Ann still tends to avoid the pronoun "I." She will use the third person instead, saying "People make mistakes" instead of "I made a mistake."

Food Note: From her earliest years, Mary Ann turned away from sweets. For her first birthday we put a candle in an English muffin rather than a cupcake or any kind of cake. A few years later we switched to cheesecake, which still is her favorite dessert. Today some autism specialists recommend a low sugar diet, with no refined carbohydrates, especially white bread. Evidently Mary Ann has deliberately chosen such a diet, at least most of the time. She even removes the buns from her hamburgers when she eats out.

Accomplishments during three years on Long Island: Mary Ann began to talk, with very primitive language, often echolalic and still reversing pronouns. Her speech involved almost exclusively nouns and a few adjectives, rarely verbs, and never other connecting words. She was, at least, beginning to initiate speech.

Mary Ann (age six), Easter in Huntington Station, Long Island

CHAPTER 3

Constipated Teddy Bears and Public School at Last

Brother Fred trying to play with Mary Ann (age seven) in Lexington, Massachusetts

In July 1971, our lives changed dramatically. At that time we made our last major move, to Lexington, Massachusetts. As usual, this move was caused by a change in George's job. As an optical engineer, George was frequently engaged in work on military contracts, designing a submarine periscope or an airplane device for night vision. He also did early research in lasers, fiber optics, and holography. Often when a contract ended, so did his job.

Had we remained in Huntington, Mary Ann would have gone to a publicly operated school for autistic children—a school with 150 children much like her, located in a renovated warehouse in the next county. I would have done what I could to resist this placement, but it would have been very difficult because still there were no laws to protect Mary Ann. We parents were just beginning to think of laws as protections and even then we were thinking more about physical safety, not protection of our children's rights, much less our rights as parents.

On Long Island and again in Massachusetts, we were paying what seemed to us astronomical real estate taxes. As Fred prepared to begin first grade, I said to George, "These taxes are paying for Fred's education, why aren't they also paying for Mary Ann's schooling?"

We decided the time had come for her to go to public school as well. Of course, like most parents in our situation, we had done a lot of research on schools for both children before settling on Lexington. I had checked out various towns and also a few private schools. Soon after we moved, I took Mary Ann to the office of Lexington's special education director and basically said to him, "Here she is. She's yours."

During our first year in Lexington, Mary Ann, now seven, attended public school for the first time, going to a special class located in the basement of one of the town's elementary schools. The seven or eight other children in the class had varying disabilities, but not autism. Without any protective laws, her class was dismissed an hour earlier than the others in the school, and periodically I would get a call from her teacher saying, "Mary Ann does not want to learn today, would you come get her and take her home?" All of this discrimination was still legal.

Through Dr. Anna Wolff, a noted psychiatrist in Cambridge, Massachusetts, we found a young psychologist, Sandy Stone, who had an interest in autism. Ms. Stone took Mary Ann on as a regular counseling patient. Using toys, she helped Mary Ann begin to understand family relationships. Like Dr. Provence and her social worker Mrs. Kirchner, Sandy Stone was using techniques to foster relationships that again, in many ways, foreshadowed the later work of Stanley Greenspan, Ruby

Salazar, and Barry Prizant.[17] At the same time, Sandy taught me a lot. For example, she helped me understand some of Mary Ann's limitations in body awareness. She taught me that when Mary Ann played with a hand puppet, she probably did not literally understand where her hand ended and the puppet began. After about two years, Sandy Stone seized an opportunity to move to England to further her education and her career. We were happy to have her for even a short time.

Around this time, Mary Ann was beginning to play more appropriately with her brother Fred. On one of our exploratory trips from Long Island to Massachusetts, in the motel where we were staying, the two children entertained each other with teddy bears suffering from diarrhea alternately with constipation—much giggling and shared fun as the teddies were given enemas.

Fred's closest school friend, Ronald Fink, has shared a couple of his recollections about Mary Ann. He recalls that the first time he came to our house, I had told Mary Ann that she could not run around without any clothes when company was there. Another time when we were driving to Boston and I slipped through a red light and was stopped by a policeman, I could not stop Mary Ann from talking—about something totally unrelated, of course—and the policeman took pity and gave me a warning. Ron remembers that I had an ashtray full of warnings but, of course, I do not remember that at all.

One thing that made Mary Ann's communication efforts so difficult was the fact that she relied heavily on echolalia, that is, verbatim repetition of phrases and even whole sentences that she heard. Parenting a child who speaks with echolalia can be a daunting experience. One day, I was driving Mary Ann somewhere after school. As I drove around a corner just a little too fast, she suddenly exclaimed, "G*d d*** son of a b***h!" I could not reprimand her very sternly because the phrase came out in my exact intonation, as if from a recording. From then on, I monitored my language closely even when I was muttering under my breath.

As early as elementary school age, Mary Ann's musical ability

---

17   Barry M. Prizant, PhD, is director of Childhood Communication Services in Cranston, Rhode Island, and adjunct professor at the Center for the Study of Human Development at Brown University. Ruby Salazar is a colleague of both Greenspan and Prizant. She is director of PA Lifespan Services and Clinical Director at the Commonwealth Medical School.

began to emerge. She sang beautifully, but we soon realized it was always someone's recording she had heard. Even now, she will sing the *Sesame Street* version of "The Twelve Days of Christmas" in the exact same voice she heard long ago on the TV show.

Not long after we moved to Lexington, I attended an autism conference in Washington DC. My mother went along with me and the two children to help take care of them. President Nixon's daughter Julie arranged to take a group of autistic children, their siblings, and parents on a tour of the White House. My mother took my two children while I was conducting business somewhere. In each room they entered, Mary Ann sat on the floor and took off her shoes and socks—much to my mother's consternation and to the amusement of one of my friends. Meanwhile all the other autistic kids, of varying ages, removed and replaced lids on all the teapots and other containers.

At the time I thought it was rather stupid of the President's family even to offer such an invitation. However, over time, I have changed that opinion. In a way, Julie Nixon was ahead of her time, inviting the children with autism to enjoy the same experience that other touring children got to have.

Today's occupational therapists could readily explain this behavior on the White House visit. Very likely, Mary Ann's feet were uncomfortable, probably too warm, and she still lacked enough language to tell anyone about it. Furthermore, like her father George, Mary Ann has always preferred no shoes and socks. The other children were probably exploring with perfectly normal curiosity, again lacking the language to ask questions. For a variety of reasons, most importantly their segregation from other children their age, none of these children had any notion that their behavior was in any way inappropriate.

When we moved from Long Island to Lexington, I decided I would no longer spend time with disability organizations—I would join the local Newcomers Club and play bridge. However, early that fall in 1971, I noticed an item in the local newspaper announcing a meeting of the Massachusetts organization representing children with autism. The name of the organization was AMIC, Association for Mentally Ill Children, another indication of the strange history of autism. In various parts of the country, these children were called mentally ill, emotionally disturbed, atypical, or suffering from childhood schizophrenia, only occasionally autistic. I later learned that those with the most severe forms of autism were usually lumped in with mentally retarded children. This history of change in terminology and placement plays a significant role in what appears to be a dramatic increase in the incidence of autism and, in fact, has made it difficult to calculate from national baseline data.

At that AMIC meeting, Barbara Cutler, a mother who soon became my close friend and mentor, presented a briefing on a bill that had just been filed in the Massachusetts legislature. It soon would become the revolutionary special education law known as Chapter 766, the Massachusetts law that preceded the federal law, now called IDEA, by three years.

Starting with Barbara's first presentation, I was spellbound by what I was hearing. This proposed law would require each "handicapped" child to be educated according to the child's individual educational needs, not simply be placed in a segregated special class or private school based on a label with no real educational meaning. The proposed law sounded so exciting that I immediately volunteered to help, and before I knew it I was spending many hours every week at the Massachusetts State House. Soon I became co-chairperson of the Massachusetts Coalition for Special Education, along with Betty Joel of the state chapter of the National Association of Social Workers. On Fridays when I left the state house, the elevator operator would say, "Have a nice weekend dear," and one time a person assigned to distribute paychecks tried to give me one. More importantly, I was getting to know the parents of children with every conceivable disability and the various professionals who served them.

Throughout the fall of 1971 and the winter and spring of 1972, many people in Boston and throughout the state worked hard to frame and enact this landmark legislation. The bill literally originated within the legislature, led by Michael Daly, House Chairman of the Education Committee, and his staff assistant, Robert Crabtree, with early support from the Speaker of the House, David Bartley, and two of his staff assistants, Peggy Maxwell and Connie Rizoli, and also from Larry Kotin who then worked for Governor Frank Sargent. It is important to note that Daly and Bartley were Democrats and that Sargent was a Republican.

Daly and Crabtree were familiar with a model special education bill developed by the Council for Exceptional Children with funding from the federal Bureau of Education for the Handicapped. In addition, they applied to special education the lessons they had learned the year before when they succeeded in enacting a pioneer bilingual education law. The most significant strategy they had learned was the importance of bringing together all the major stakeholders, and building a strong coalition at the beginning of the process.

In the fall of 1971, Massachusetts, like many other states, had in place a variety of separate laws for children with disabilities, with each law designed for children with a particular disability: a law for deaf children, one for blind children, one for mentally retarded, the most recent one for children with learning disabilities, and one for emotionally disturbed children (known as Chapter 750), which included autistic children. Since these laws varied greatly, a child needed to be born with the "right" disability in order to get services, and heaven forbid if a child had more than one problem—say deaf and autistic or mentally retarded and mobility impaired. Parents were organized around the various specific disabilities and they had worked hard to achieve any education at all for their group of children, so it was not easy to bring together all the various disability groups to support a single law that would bring equity and quality to all children no matter what the disability or label assigned to the child.

By this time I realized that not all autistic children were like Mary Ann. Furthermore, I soon learned that similar kinds of variety occur within all the disabilities, and that there is usually more variation within a disability group than there is between disabilities, especially as far as educational needs are concerned. This reality is so well-known and accepted today that it is hard to believe how entrenched the opposite view was in 1971, not just in Massachusetts but throughout the country.

Food note: During her first seven years, Mary Ann essentially ate whatever food was put before her, unlike many children, including those with autism, who often develop narrow, specific food choices. She ate fruit and vegetables but only if they accompanied meat or fish.

In Connecticut I had learned a great way to prepare swordfish—a new taste sensation for me, having grown up in Indiana with only freshwater fish. Mary Ann loved it and she still does. Here is the recipe:

- Select a piece of swordfish approximately one inch thick. Rub each side with a half clove of garlic. Add salt and pepper.
- Spread butter over each side of the fish.
- Place in an oven-proof dish and then nearly cover it with milk, any version of milk—whole, skim, or in between.
- Put the fish in a broiler set at 350 degrees and cook for about twenty minutes.
- When done and slightly brown, move the fish to a serving platter and garnish with parsley or other fresh green herb.

Throughout these years, Mary Ann refused to drink water and she did not develop a taste for soda—partly because George and I did not encourage it—until much later as an adult. She drank only fruit juice. Even now she still prefers a glass of wine or beer, coffee, and then finally, some water.

Milestones: Mary Ann slowly developed more spoken language, though still strange, with lots of echolalia, an unusual use of pronouns, and heavy reliance on nouns. She was also developing some artistic abilities and she began to sing in her school chorus.

Chapter 4

"Where's the Meat?"

During the time I was working hard to change state and federal special education laws, Mary Ann was talking more and more but still not communicating clearly. Her speech continued to rely heavily on echolalia—verbatim repetition of phrases, whole sentences, and sometimes a half-hour mixture of my telephone calls and the TV show, *Sesame Street*. Big Bird and Bert and Ernie were interspersed with Peggy Maxwell, Bob Crabtree, and Barbara Cutler. While such a recitation seemed to play no communicative function, it did give Mary Ann great pleasure. Around this time she also developed a superb imitation of Julia Child, from her television show, *The French Chef*, and she was learning to appreciate praise and/or amusement from her listeners.

Children in our neighborhood basically ignored Mary Ann. Some of the parents made overtures to include her; some did not. Looking back, I realize this behavior probably was based more on uncertainty and bewilderment than on deliberate efforts at exclusion. When Mary Ann was a child in elementary school, autism was essentially unheard of—the term and the disorder did not penetrate the awareness of the general public until the movie *Rainman* was released in 1988. It is amazing to me how that one movie brought autism out of the closet and stimulated interest among so many people who had no direct involvement with the disorder. Strangers took an interest in Mary Ann simply because she was a real live version of Dustin Hoffman's character.

Mary Ann is carnivorous. I often wish I could have a talk with Dr. Haake, the pediatrician in Rochester, who said to me when Mary Ann was about a year old, "Let her have all the meat she wants." At times I have felt like sending that doctor my meat bill for just one month.

My daughter appears to believe the worst handicap anyone could have is being a vegetarian. I have barely survived many a situation when Mary Ann cried piteously, "Where's the meat? Is this meal vegetarian?" She has done this since her middle teens, when she first had enough language to express it clearly, until her mid-thirties. She has now learned just enough social skills to express her complaints with a certain amount of discretion, but she still does not like a vegetarian meal. Recently I was able to explain to her that vegetable lasagna would be OK because it contains cheese, which is part of the "meat group." With some skepticism she ate it. That experience made me wonder whether her obsession with meat is an actual taste requirement or whether it comes from constant teaching about the four food groups. Perhaps both.

Temple Grandin would disagree.[18] In her book *Animals in Translation,* Grandin discusses the evolution of humans as meat eaters. She observes that people on the autism spectrum may have an even stronger preference for meat than other people do, and that they may have a genetically wired need for meat.

This strong preference may stem at least partially from another aspect of biology—some researchers have found that many children with autism do best on a diet high in protein and low in refined carbohydrates. As I said earlier, from a very early age Mary Ann refused food laden with sugar.

Over the years, Mary Ann was subjected to many, many IQ tests—most of them absolutely useless or misleading or both. However, when she was nine, I was able to arrange for Dr. Janet Brown, a psychologist at the Judge Baker Children's Center at Harvard Medical School, to come to our house to test Mary Ann. Instead of playing the role of "apple-cheeked Vassar girl," as one of my friends used to say, Dr. Brown was totally unconventional in her approach and relied on her own knowledge and experience. She administered portions of four different tests and found that Mary Ann tested from three years to nine years, depending on the kind of test, in other words which skills were being measured. This was the only valid IQ test Mary Ann ever had.

---

18   Temple Grandin is the best-known autistic self-advocate in this country. She has written several books and she is a professor in the Department of Animal Science at Colorado State University, Fort Collins.

Interestingly, this test predated Howard Gardner's work on multiple intelligences.

At one point during Mary Ann's elementary school years, we were able to secure piano lessons for her with a talented music therapist for one year, before the teacher moved to New Hampshire. It was already clear that Mary Ann loved to sing and that she had a lovely singing voice, and the teacher took advantage of this talent. She would have Mary Ann work hard at the keyboard for about ten minutes and then let her sing a song, accompanying her on a guitar. Then it was back to work again for another ten minutes, another singing break, and a final five minutes or so of work at the keyboard.

For her first three years in Lexington (1971–74), Mary Ann was placed in a "special class" that moved from one elementary school building to another each year. For one year, by sheer chance, her class was located in her neighborhood school, but then it moved again, this time staying put for three years. Mary Ann quickly learned to adjust to the changes involved in moving to different school buildings in Lexington. By the third move, she was learning to sing in the chorus, participate a little on the regular playground, and generally learn school behavior and participation.

In this third location, Mary Ann finally had the services of a well-qualified special education teacher, Suella Horner. Suella used a variety of teaching techniques with the children and when she found that one technique was not working, she turned to another. One very effective device she used was a daily communication notebook between school and home.

Suella Horner did everything she could to involve her students in the total school program. At one point she realized it was counterproductive having her class, with its special kitchen equipment and special doorway, located at the far end of the building. She sacrificed the special equipment in order to move the class into the center of the building where her children would have much easier access to the other children and teachers. She also arranged for Mary Ann to sing with the "regular" fourth graders in their chorus.

CHAPTER 5
Inclusion at Last, for a While

In the fall of 1977, Mary Ann made the move from elementary school to Clarke Junior High School. By that time, special education practices in Lexington had improved even more and now Mary Ann was about to benefit from a truly effective program. At Clarke, we encountered another talented special educator, Joan Thormann, who had her doctorate from the University of Oregon.[19] After working with Mary Ann for a short time in the resource room, Joan concluded that Mary Ann should be "mainstreamed"—the term being used at the time, before "inclusion" had entered our vocabulary—with her age peers. Joan persuaded the reluctant principal and "regular" academic teachers, some of whom were resistant, to try mainstreaming Mary Ann.

Clarke Junior High School was departmentalized and operated with a tracking system—three levels of students, based on ability. Joan Thormann chose to place Mary Ann in the highest-performing section of each subject because she realized these students would be the least threatened by her presence. Joan provided information and basic training to the receiving teachers and, by and large, they were happy to try it. When Joan addressed one of the classes, a student asked her, "What should we do if Mary Ann drops to the floor, yelling?" Joan's commonsense reply was "Don't let her."

Mary Ann quickly learned to navigate movement from one classroom to another throughout the day in the large junior high school. The one time I spent a day there visiting and observing, I was exhausted before the last class of the day, but not Mary Ann.

---

19   Joan Thormann is now Professor of Technology in Education at Lesley University.

33

Soon Mary Ann discovered that her new friends were learning Spanish and she wanted to join them. When Joan raised this possibility with me, I was reluctant because of Mary Ann's limited English mastery, but Joan talked me into letting Mary Ann try it. It turned out to be one of the best things that happened in her entire educational life. (At the time, one of my friends told me that almost all mentally retarded children in Europe learn a second language.) Eventually I realized this important step took advantage of one of Mary Ann's major autistic characteristics, the ability to memorize verbatim. Now she could practice her echolalia with impunity. She could be praised for it rather than criticized.

Contrary to everything I had been told while studying to become a teacher of both Latin and English, learning a second language opened Mary Ann's eyes and mind to language in general. Suddenly she discovered new levels of meaning in language and in words, and she was full of excitement about this discovery. She began to ask the meaning of words, a major advance for her, and she continues to do this into her mid-forties. For instance, she recently asked me, "What does perseveration mean?"

One day after a trip to Disneyland in Anaheim a few days before Halloween, Mary Ann and I went to a Mexican restaurant for supper. As soon as the waiter arrived at our table, Mary Ann asked him, "What is the Spanish for 'Halloween'?" The restaurant was full of cobwebs, witches, and ghosts, but the waiter did not know the answer. Still, good waitperson that he was, he scurried around the restaurant inquiring and finally got the words from one of the cooks: *fiesta que se celebra el día 31 de octubre, víspera de la festividad de Todos los Santos.* I later learned that there is no single word in Spanish for Halloween because the Hispanic countries do not celebrate that holiday as we do. Needless to say, the waiter received a good tip.

I took Mary Ann and my mother along on another trip to Southern California for a conference. After the meeting, we added a few days of vacation, along with my colleague Judith Raskin, proceeding to San Diego and then on to the Baja Peninsula. As we pulled into Tijuana, a young boy of about ten motioned to us, offering to find us a parking space. I was quite sure that I could find an empty parking space on my own, but I decided to play the game. As I was parking the car, a second, older and bigger boy came along and as we were getting out, the two

of them started arguing, probably over who would get the tip and how large it should be. Suddenly Mary Ann cheerfully said, "Hola!"

In a split second those two boys vanished and neither got the hoped-for tip. The situation was ironic in several ways because of so much they could not realize. Mary Ann was the only person in our party who spoke Spanish. She could care less what mischief they were discussing—she was just happy to come across two people close to her age with whom she could speak Spanish. By running off, they had unwittingly been hurtful to a person with a disability.

As I mentioned earlier, around the time Mary Ann began junior high school, she was accepted as a patient by the clinical psychologist and researcher Dr. William Condon. By filming people with autism, Dr. Condon had demonstrated that they experience a longer-than-usual delay between a sound stimulus and their response to it. Ralph Maurer, Anne Donellan, and others later incorporated his observations as they developed theories of autism as a neurologically based movement disorder.

In addition to his work on autistic people's processing of sound, Dr. Condon also became more and more of an expert in studying and explaining many of the peculiarities of autistic language—helping to explain misunderstandings and also misuse of language. He taught me how to study and understand Mary Ann's fundamentally metaphorical language. For instance, in the course of her therapy with Dr. Condon, Mary Ann developed a role-play story about Gloria the washing machine. (She has always been obsessed with washing machines and laundromats, as I discuss in detail in the next chapter.) Occasionally, Gloria would "go off balance" and then would be punished—sent away. Dr. Condon and I together deduced that this description was a metaphor for being handicapped or not "talking right." Throughout her life she had been constantly corrected with her use of language. At one point Gloria acquired a boyfriend, Ralph, who was a car. Periodically Ralph had a flat tire—another metaphor for a handicapping condition.

Food note: By the time Mary Ann attended junior high school, I had little time for gardening. However, I always managed to grow a few tomatoes and fresh herbs, at least sweet basil. As a follower of the *New York Times* food writer Craig Claiborne, I had found a marvelous use for my homegrown basil, a recipe for pesto sauce: Basil, olive oil, garlic

cloves, pinch of salt. Mary Ann quickly acquired a taste for it. Now in her mid-forties, when she goes to an Italian restaurant she invariably orders a side of pesto sauce.

Milestones: Three years of inclusion in regular classes in junior high school were enormously successful for Mary Ann. She participated in art, chorus, history and English classes, typing, and Spanish. One of her history teachers was especially skilled—he would teach a class as usual and then, during the last ten minutes, when the other students were planning their next assignment, he would come to Mary Ann and go over with her the parts of the lesson he thought she could understand. Nearly all of her teachers were very proud of her accomplishments; I felt many of them had discovered skills they did not know they had.

Mary Ann's typing teacher was so proud of her. I think he predicted she would become the first autistic bilingual typist at the United Nations.

CHAPTER 6
High School Challenge

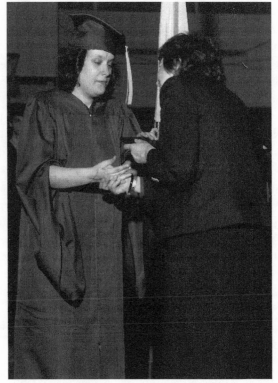

High school graduation, Mary Ann receiving her diploma

The transition to high school was another big challenge. One of the administrators thought Mary Ann should go to the regional vocational technical high school. Today that might be a viable choice, but at the time she would have had to give up further classes in Spanish and also singing in a chorus in exchange for vocational training. This situation presented a tough dilemma. After careful thought and conversation with many people, including Mary Ann herself, we decided to send her to the regular high school.

By this time, we had moved to a house much closer to the center of town and also closer to the high school. Finally, Mary Ann was able to walk to school, thus achieving a goal she had long aspired to. She had developed a hearty dislike for the little yellow special buses she had been forced to rely on for so many years.

Allowing Mary Ann to walk to school, eight blocks away, across one of Lexington's busiest streets, presented new tests for our changing views of protection. It did not help that Lexington, like so many modern suburban towns, had very few sidewalks. Even so, the basics of pedestrian safety were relatively simple, but then came the question of her being offered rides in cars. I knew that telling her not to ride with a "stranger" was not the answer—"stranger" is an abstract term, open to many different interpretations. Finally, I decided to do this one backwards. I said to her, "Mary Ann, if people offer you a ride in the car, only get in these cars: Mom's, Dad's, or Mrs. Calvin's, Page's mom. Do not get in any other car." (Page is a friend who had been in Mary Ann's elementary school class and her mother worked at the high school.) Mary Ann knew many other people in Lexington, but this short list seemed the best solution. Most importantly, it worked.

At this time, Lexington High School had the bare beginnings of a special education program in spite of the new laws. This may have been a blessing in disguise since it meant there was no easy place to segregate Mary Ann. She continued Spanish for two more years and she sang in the high school chorus.

She soon indicated she wanted to take a science course. This request threw everyone for a loop. Her teachers and administrators wanted to honor her request but they also wanted to protect her from dismal failure. For two consecutive years she was signed up for a low-level course in indoor gardening. Not too surprisingly, each fall that course was dropped because too few students signed for it. Finally, someone had the brilliant idea of placing Mary Ann in first-year biology. With some trepidation, I went along with this choice. This turned out to be an excellent move. Mary Ann flourished and the biology teacher was very proud of her.

Eventually I realized that biology was a good choice because it relied on Mary Ann's ability to memorize verbatim, a talent shared with many autistic people.

Once Mary Ann was integrated into regular classes in junior high school, she began to sing in the school chorus and continued to do that through high school. Not only did she enjoy the music and contribute musically, she also was learning "chorus behavior," especially the importance of carefully following the direction of the teacher. When I learned that the high school had a smaller singing group called "Girls' Ensemble," I approached the music teacher who ran the group to encourage her to include Mary Ann. The teacher was very reluctant, clearly not wanting Mary Ann there. Unfortunately for her, I had attended enough concerts by then that I knew what poor singers some of the other members were; I refused to give in. Soon Mary Ann was included and she blended right in, making a major contribution to the quality of the music.

During these years, Mary Ann continued to benefit some from her inclusion with other students her age and she participated a little in regular classes. However, she was not really learning much in the way of vocational preparation. She did work a few hours each week cleaning equipment and organizing the space in the nurse's office. This activity pleased her. She also was not on a track to fulfill the requirements for a high school diploma as she was lacking in math plus a few other academic courses. Math was an impossible challenge for Mary Ann throughout her school years and later. It is easy for all of us, parents and teachers, to forget how abstract math is as a subject. By now, I hope schools have developed some techniques for overcoming this challenge.

By the time Mary Ann's twentieth birthday drew near, I began to feel it was no longer appropriate for her to be going to school with sixteen-year-olds. I had known all along about a totally segregated vocational program for students with special needs located at one end of the Lexington High School campus. This was a program known as LABB (Lexington, Arlington, Bedford, Burlington), a regional collaborative vocational program serving students from Lexington and several neighboring towns.

After extensive argument with myself, I decided it was time for Mary Ann to move from the high school to a vocational program. Her transitional IEP team agreed with me and she then moved to LABB for the final two years of her education. There she had a chance to go to work in an enclave—a group of people with disabilities working together in an ordinary workplace—at Honeywell. She learned appropriate work behavior and was able to participate in the LABB recreation program. Ultimately she did receive a diploma, with a waiver, and at the graduation ceremony she was roundly applauded—in spite of her autism, she had made many friends.

During her adolescence, Mary Ann learned to swim, taking lessons at a local private recreation center. By the time she graduated from high school, she was swimming laps once a week at Hayden Recreation Center and she is by far the best swimmer in our family. In summer she would walk to the nearby pond and later to the town pool to go swimming. When she travels with me, she insists on staying at a motel with a pool.

Betsy Anderson, a friend and colleague, remembers the days when Mary Ann would occasionally come with me to work at our office in Boston. Betsy remembers that Mary Ann would become very anxious if I continued to talk on the telephone and lunch got later and later. Mary Ann would ask anxiously, "Will we skip a meal today?" This still happens occasionally. Betsy further remembers that on the elevator going down to the lunch room, Mary Ann, still anxious, would ask "Will this be vegetarian?" At the time, Betsy recalls that she wondered whether Mary Ann feared that she might "catch" vegetarianism, and that she probably did not understand that people often consciously decide to eat a vegetarian meal or become vegetarian. This was, and is, a personal, intimate aspect of her flawed understanding of cause and effect.

When Betsy and I recall these questions, we remember they were not uttered just once—they were repeated many times, often with increasing intensity.

Autistic children often do have special food cravings and not always for meat. Mary Ann's friend Keith craved sweets, even plain, granulated sugar. His family had to hide and lock up everything sweet, including the bag of sugar, or Keith would get into it and devour great quantities of it.

Mary Ann has always been fascinated by brightly colored lights. When she was a child, she would literally dance around the Christmas tree when she first saw it all lit up and decorated. George and I would carefully put it up either after she went to bed or while she was napping, because her reaction to the newly decorated tree was always so delicious—her eyes glistened and she clapped her hands as she danced around.

On a trip to Puerto Rico, my mother, Mary Ann, and I had dinner at a restaurant on the Condado, the famous tourist street along the beach in San Juan. Unfortunately for my mother and me, the dining room had a multicolored rotating light in the center of the ceiling. Mary Ann was transfixed by the moving beams of colored light. She stood in the center of the restaurant, staring at them and humming. She was about fifteen and had started to learn Spanish, but she was clearly too old to be engaged in such childish behavior. She had not yet learned the meaning of the word "appropriate," and neither had I learned the potency of that term. I tried everything I could think of to distract her, but nothing worked. She could not even concentrate on her food.

Grandma and I suffered through as best we could, neither of us knowing any Spanish to help explain the situation to the waitress or the other customers. After the meal, Mary Ann was distraught at having to leave the restaurant with its seductive light. As we slowly strolled up the Condado, trying to relax, Grandma said, "Mary Ann, think happy thoughts." I struggled not to laugh at such an absurd thing to say to a young teenager with autism, but as I think back, I realize that the soothing tone of my mother's voice probably did help calm Mary Ann.

She is, in fact, very sensitive to the tone of people's voices. In 1980, when the late Senator Edward Kennedy was seeking the Democratic nomination for President, I took Mary Ann along to a state conference of the Massachusetts Association for Retarded Citizens, where he gave a keynote address. At that time, he was campaigning hard for a strengthened treaty banning nuclear weapons, and he spoke very sternly about the threat of nuclear war.

After the speech, as the Senator and his aides were leaving the hall, I took Mary Ann to meet him. She asked him loudly and insistently, "Why are you angry?" He was quite taken aback. Several months later, my friend Janet Vohs showed me an article about Senator Kennedy in

Rolling Stone magazine that recounted that episode. The writer indicated that as a result of Mary Ann's question, Senator Kennedy actually toned down his speaking style.

Not only is Mary Ann's reaction to Senator Kennedy's tone of voice significant, his reaction to her question is equally significant. He did not brush off her response as nothing important, or as coming from an inferior person. Rather, he immediately accepted her comment as genuine and full of meaning for him personally.

Like so many people on the autism spectrum, Mary Ann's sensory experiences and her reaction to them are often unpredictable, even shocking sometimes. On March 21, in 1984, when Mary Ann was twenty, I received a phone call from a teacher at Mary Ann's vocational program. The woman scolded me for allowing Mary Ann to go to school without a coat. The outdoor temperature was in the thirties. By that time, Mary Ann was quite independent and got herself up and out in the morning, walking about a mile to school. I was probably in the shower when she left. It took a lot of detective work to figure out what had happened, but eventually George and I realized that she had indeed walked to school with no coat because it was the first day of spring! Furthermore, I suspect she did not feel the cold all that much either—an example of "mind over matter."

Milestones: Although Mary Ann did not learn as much as she should have academically during these final years of school, she did acquire some other important skills. She became steadily more independent, walking to school on her own, for instance. She learned that she herself could make some choices and not just tolerate those offered by her parents. She also discovered that she too could make a contribution through work.

CHAPTER 7
Beginning of Adult Life

Mary Ann in her adult residence in Lexington

Mary Ann continues to surprise me. A few years ago at Christmas time, a widely advertised toy was a life-size parrot that contained a built-in tape recorder enabling the parrot to repeat exactly what you said to it. I thought, "Ah ha! Now Mary Ann can begin to learn what it feels like when someone continually repeats the same sentence, usually a question, over and over and is never satisfied with the answer."

I got her the parrot for Christmas, but she outsmarted me. One day as I passed her bedroom I overheard her talking. When I went in, I discovered she had placed the parrot on her bed and was teaching it Spanish. The parrot was learning it really well too.

Through her counselor, Dr. William Condon, I have learned new ways to think about her intense repetition of questions. He taught me that she repeats her questions incessantly because she is not getting the right answer. Actually, she is not getting the answer to the right question because she has used a personal metaphor that is clear only to her. For example, "Will we have a power failure?" can mean, "Will something really bad happen?" I suspect this is an instance where she herself is converting an abstract question into a concrete example.

Mary Ann loves role-playing and this is a very effective learning technique for her and for those of us who are trying to understand her better. She first experienced role-playing at age eleven, when she attended a six-week summer program, Camp Freedom in New Hampshire. Bruce Baker, then a psychology professor at Harvard, ran the program.

Frequently, during a session with Dr. Condon, she would say "Let's role-play." She will make this request often for what appears to be sheer fun, and other times she does it in order to work through a problem she has experienced, often with one of her housemates or with staff.

Occasionally, Mary Ann asks to role-play a situation in a restaurant. This role-play usually is benign, although sometimes she eats too fast and too much and she uses role-playing to try to improve her restaurant behavior. She also asks me to role-play with her, often when I am driving on a crowded highway. I think she sometimes does this because she is bored.

As a mature adult, Mary Ann continues to experience her own idiosyncratic physical pleasures—her own personal responses to her sensory experiences. Each summer, on one or two Saturday afternoons, Mary Ann and I go to Nantasket Beach in Hull, Massachusetts. There we ride on the antique Paragon Park carousel, lovingly saved and restored by local businesses and citizens. Mary Ann has always enjoyed riding on a merry-go-round—whether in Golden Gate Park in San Francisco, Disneyland, or at the annual Fourth of July carnival in Lexington. She always sits on the bench, not on the horses or other animals that move up and down. In fact, she is incensed if a new carousel has no benches. The Paragon Park carousel is all right, even though the bench takes the form of a chariot. Clearly, the important point is that it is stationary, and not moving up and down.

As soon as the music begins and the carousel starts to move, a look of absolute bliss spreads over Mary Ann's face. Evidently the feeling of the centrifugal force, combined with the music, has an almost intoxicating effect on her. I am often reminded of Temple Grandin's comments, in her first book, *Emergence: Labeled Autistic,* about how she enjoyed the Cyclone, a carnival ride with even greater centrifugal force. I continue to be curious about this particular love of Mary Ann's. What does it tell me about her, in addition to her obvious pleasure? What does it tell us about autism or other neurological disabilities? The late Gunnar Dybwad, professor at Brandeis University, once suggested that Mary Ann's pleasure on the carousel may be enhanced by the fact that she has a degree of control over it. That is, *she* decides when to get on and where to sit.

One Saturday when I took Mary Ann to Nantasket Beach, the carousel was crowded. She patiently checked out the stationary seats and finally sat down beside a young man somewhat younger than she who was accompanied by an older man who appeared to be his father. I quickly surmised that this young man was also autistic. At the end of the ride I inquired briefly and I was right. That experience had me thinking, how could we provide a similar experience for Mary Ann and others like her that would be more age appropriate? Or could someone simply design stationary seats that have a more grownup appearance? Meanwhile, Mary Ann could care less. She loves to ride on a carousel, whether at Nantasket Beach, at the annual Lions Club Carnival in Lexington, or at a county fair in Indiana.

For a very long time, Mary Ann has been fascinated by washing machines and dryers, especially the machines that spin around behind a glass door. The comic-strip character, Zippy the Pinhead, drew a correlation between watching TV and watching clothes turning in a dryer window—it is something that mesmerizes many ordinary people. Even now, as an adult, she will comment on a laundromat that she spots as we are driving. Recently when I asked her why she is so interested in laundromats, she eventually indicated that she is attracted to the spinning. Perhaps just seeing or thinking about the spinning gives her some of the intoxicating sensation she experiences on the carousel.

One time when our family went to visit George's sister and her husband in Philadelphia, we pulled up in front of the wrong house—a similar brick house but a block away. Before I had time to discover our mistake, Mary Ann had entered the house and found the washing machine. At that time, whenever we visited friends or relatives she needed to locate the laundry equipment immediately, but this occurrence was truly extreme, she completely ignored the fact that the residents were total strangers. All that mattered to her were their washer and dryer.

Through Kristi Koenig, a professor of occupational therapy at Temple University, and David Schwartz, a psychologist and author, I have learned the term "optokenetic nystagmus," the technical term for the motion of the eyes following moving objects. Both think there is something special about this characteristic in many people on the autism spectrum. It would account for Mary Ann's love of the carousel, as well as the visual experience of a spinning washing machine.

One year the company that operates the annual Lexington Lions Club carnival failed to set up a merry-go-round. *Disaster.* Especially for our family. When I inquired, I was told that one of the carousels was being repaired and the other one was being used on Cape Cod. This explanation was absolutely unacceptable to Mary Ann. In desperation, I finally decided to use this experience as a lesson in self-advocacy. At my urging and assistance, Mary Ann wrote a letter of protest to the Lexington Lions Club. She did not get a reply, but the carousel has never again been missing.

Recently, in my work at Youth Advocate Programs Inc. in Pennsylvania, I have been learning a lot about sensory problems in children and adults with autism. My main teachers have been Moya Kinnealey, chairman of the occupational therapy department at Temple University, and her colleague Kristi Koenig. I have also learned a lot from Bill Stillman, an adult with Asperger Syndrome who has been busy writing, speaking, and teaching.[20] When I learned how difficult it can be for autistic people to catch a ball because of their uncertainty about their bodies in space, I thought about one of Mary Ann's favorite games. She loves to toss a Frisbee for a dog to chase and return, and she is very good at doing this. Her favorite dog partner was the late Dingo, who lived with Mary Ann's Aunt Mary in Champagne-Urbana,

---

20   See Bill's article in *Huffington Post* (September 9, 2009), "Autism: The Last Human Rights Movement" and his Web page, www.williamstillman.com for a list of his publications and presentation topics.

and Dingo also thought Mary Ann was terrific. While engaging in this game, Mary Ann did not need to worry about catching an object hurtling toward her. Instead, Dingo dutifully brought the Frisbee and more or less handed it to her.

For several years, Mary Ann, like a couple of million other people, loved to go to ballgames at Fenway Park, home of the Boston Red Sox. The first time I took her there was for the last game played by Carl Yaztremski, iconic outfielder for the Red Sox. What a thrill to watch Yaz circle the park several times, waving a bottle of champagne, saying farewell to his Boston fans. It was a terrific treat for me and for my son, Fred. Mary Ann, who did not quite understand the specialness of the day, fell in love with baseball, and with baseball players.

First she became enamored of a second baseman, whose name I have forgotten, who was soon traded. But then she fell in love with the great Roger Clemens, and I said to myself, "Good. You have raised this girl right." (Later my views of Roger Clemens changed some.)

Finally, of course, the Boston Red Sox, in their great wisdom, let Roger Clemens get away. Mary Ann has not talked about this change, but I suspect she thinks it is a lot like the constant turnover of staff at her work program and at her group home—just get to know and like someone and off that person goes, never to be heard from again. Little did I realize at the time, but the ritual farewell to and from Yaz may have been one of the last such sentimental partings of a great baseball player, at least at Fenway Park.

For several years, Mary Ann went to Fenway Park once each summer with some nondisabled friends, who always get tickets for a Yankees game. However, she now talks more about football. Perhaps football players demand less of the loyalty that will ultimately be betrayed—as big anonymous hunks who run and knock each other down, they are unidentifiable behind the helmets and the padding.

As a living illustration of the writing of Temple Grandin and the teaching of Alex Michaels and other adults on the autism spectrum, Mary Ann has always loved to draw, color, and paint pictures.[21] Early

---

21   Alex Michaels, who lives with Asperger syndrome, founded and heads Advancing Milestones Inc. in Waltham, MA. She has developed a curriculum on Asperger's for UMass Medical Center and was featured in a *National Geographic* magazine center page in July 1999. She is unequaled in her ability to explain the experience of Asperger syndrome and its relative, autism.

on, Dr. Condon recognized these as communicating a lot about Mary Ann, her feelings especially. I vividly remember her painting "Angry Fish" and also one of a girl standing on the edge of a roof, hands outstretched, either ready to jump or simply scared nearly to death.

If I bring Mary Ann with me to a conference or a meeting, I always bring along plenty of paper and either crayons or magic markers. She will relieve her boredom by drawing pictures. One of my favorites is a black and white drawing of a Christmas tree. The tree is covered with the usual round ornaments, but the color of each one is labeled, in Spanish as well as English. Furthermore, in the large number of ornaments, there is no duplication of colors. She did not learn this device from me—unlike many people, I have never been a doodler and, in fact, neither was George.

Is this the activity of a mentally retarded person? There is an active, focused, knowledgeable mind at work here. It is one more example of the irrelevance of the term "mentally retarded," not just for autistic people but for anyone.

The first time Mary Ann came with me as a co-presenter at a workshop, we worked together to prepare an introductory statement from her. Then a high school student, at one point she said, "Elementary school made me retarded." That brief statement conveyed a whole lot about her early education and her thoughts about it. It was true that she was in a small, segregated class within a regular elementary school building, and while our family never used the term "retarded" with her, she undoubtedly heard it from other children in the school, perhaps even from some of her classmates.

Furthermore, in some ways, she was literally correct. In a small, segregated class for all those years, she was learning little of the material that elementary school children usually learn, including geography, history, and literature. For me, her remark was a vivid reminder both of the progress we have made in educating our children with special needs and simultaneously the journey still before us to reach the hope promised in our laws and constantly changing philosophy.

In thinking about Mary Ann's thoughts and feelings about her disability, I am reminded of observations by two friends. In June 2005, *Sports Illustrated* magazine ran a story about my friend Dick Hoyt and his son, Rick, who has severe cerebral palsy. Every year, Dick pushes Rick in his special wheelchair in the Boston marathon. (Rick is now an adult and a graduate of Boston University.) When the interviewer asked Dick why he undertook such a rigorous endeavor and continues it to this day, even after his own retirement, Dick replied that after he pushed Rick in a much shorter race to help a childhood friend, Rick commented with his computer, "Dad, when we were running, it felt like I wasn't disabled anymore."

My friend Harvey Liebergott, in his book *Scissors, Rock, Paper*[22] about his experience with martial arts, writes about "no mindedness," a rare spiritual state of euphoric disconnect from the physical world that is, ironically, achieved through disciplined physical endeavor. I have often thought Mary Ann's experience while swimming and also while singing must be like this, and the same applies to Rick Hoyt's sensation when his father is pushing him in a race and probably to Dick as well.

Mary Ann's sense of humor, combined with her autistic determination and ritual, sometimes enables her to really fool people. One time in junior high school, she developed a story about how our family, along with really extended family and probably friends, was planning a trip to Brazil. Her teacher, Joan Thormann, spoke to me about it and with complete credulity asked me when the trip was planned and whether we had chartered a plane. Of course I had heard nothing about it.

When Mary Ann was twenty-six, she began to sing in a local choir, at the Church of Our Redeemer in Lexington center, where she has been warmly welcomed and fully included. She loves music of all kinds. She listens to the Metropolitan Opera most Saturday afternoons, and to rock and roll, and jazz, and she loves rap. She was thrilled when I took her to the Andrew Lloyd Webber show, *Cats*, at a Boston theater.

Dr. Condon has suggested that Mary Ann feels a stronger sense of belonging when she is singing in the choir than at any other time, perhaps because language is not there as a barrier; she is "equally" participating. Occasionally Mary Ann asks me, "Why don't you and Fred go to church?" Her brother Fred has suggested that she wishes we could share this experience of belonging or perhaps she simply means, "Why don't you sing in a choir?" When summer comes and the choir goes on vacation for three months, Mary Ann stays home on Sunday mornings. Occasionally when she comments, "I miss the choir," I

---

22   Peabody Publishing Company, 1996.

suggest to her that she go to church and sit in the congregation, but she always declines. Though both George and I always loved classical music, including the religious music of Handel, Bach, Mozart, and others, we are not a church-going family.

When Mary Ann was thirty-seven, she began voice lessons with Robert Gartside, a superb voice teacher who is retired from Boston University's music department, where he chaired the voice division. At each of the first two lessons, she wanted to sing the "Hallelujah Chorus" from Handel's *Messiah*. After the second request, I suddenly realized that I needed to intervene or she would quickly embed this number into every lesson. Thinking quickly, I suggested that today, instead of the "Hallelujah Chorus," why not sing "Joyful, Joyful We Adore Thee"? She responded enthusiastically, "That's my favorite song—the Fourth Movement of the Beethoven Ninth, Opus 125." Bob Gartside and I looked at each other in amazement, and I told him we had better not argue, that she was almost certainly correct about the opus number. Sure enough, when I got home that evening, I looked it up and learned that it is indeed Opus 125. So far as I know, no one had ever mentioned this fact to her; she must have seen it on a record label or on the cover of the music.

"That's my favorite song" is a frequent, enthusiastic comment for music that Mary Ann likes. She has not learned to say, or understand, the concept of "*one* of my favorite songs." Apparently it is time for me, or someone else, to explain this distinction to her.

One day as we were driving along a highway, Mary Ann asked me, "How is Beethoven doing?" I was startled, of course—amazed that she had no idea when he had lived and died. But that was an intriguing question. She must have been wondering when he would produce his next symphony or concerto. Her question is an interesting example of what happened back in the days of segregated classes for children with disabilities, including Mary Ann, when they were excluded from the regular curriculum. I suddenly realized that Mary Ann has a distorted view of time and history, partly because she has been taught so little history of any kind. I was reminded again that, in a way, she lives in an eternal present. Soon after Mary Ann's autism was identified, my friend June Burke commented to me that there must be an "existential" aspect to her experience.

Throughout her life, Mary Ann has had great difficulty accepting any kind of vague or indefinite answer to her questions. If she asked, "When will we go home?" it was not acceptable to say, "In a little while"—she would continue to repeat the question. With the help of her counselor, Dr. Condon, and one of her teachers, I finally realized it is better to give her a precise answer, like, "We will go home at 3:30"—even if I am not certain it is correct and if it turns out not to be accurate.

In July 1988, when Mary Ann was twenty-four, George was diagnosed with cancer of the stomach and esophagus. Within a few weeks, after tests at Dana Farber Cancer Institute in Boston, we were told there was no hope. George was offered palliative chemotherapy and, if he chose, he would receive hospice services at home. He did indeed choose hospice. I explained this awful situation first to Fred and then to Mary Ann. Fred was living in an apartment in Somerville and Mary Ann was still living at home with us in Lexington.

Throughout the next three months of George's steady decline, Mary Ann never said or did anything in the least inappropriate. She seemed to be imitating the manner and behavior she observed in Fred and me and various visitors. It helped, I'm sure, that she was in a new supported employment program, at CMARC (Central Middlesex Association for Retarded Citizens).[23]

Early in September we began hospice care, setting up a hospital bed for George in the first floor bedroom. He had his faithful computer by his side. George was an optical engineer and he was in the midst of developing a new optical design program when he became ill. He loved astronomy and he cheerfully shared that knowledge and love with Fred and Mary Ann. Mary Ann probably still knows all the major constellations and most of the brightest stars by their Greek names.

George died on October 24, 1988, just three months after his initial diagnosis. For Mary Ann, that date is the single most important one, after her own birthday. If I forget, she still reminds me to take her to the cemetery on that date.

---

23   CMARC has recently changed its name to Nupath Inc.

CHAPTER 8

"Mom, I've Had Enough of You!"
Challenges of Adult Life

Mary Ann and mother Martha

Today, as families, we are living in the middle of a paradox that makes it ever harder to do the right thing for our offspring with disabilities. Throughout their school life, we place higher and higher expectations on them and insist that others, especially educators, share our high expectations. We want them to achieve to their highest possible potential, to prepare for a life of independence and productivity. Then, suddenly, when they become adults and leave school, still needing supports, we must describe them in the most harrowing possible terms, emphasizing their deficits in order for them to qualify for any kind of state or federally funded adult services, whether Supplemental Security Income (SSI), Medicaid, Social Security Disability Insurance (SSDI) Social Security Survivors Benefits, vocational rehabilitation, or housing assistance. In addition, they must be careful not to earn too much as they work in normal jobs or they will lose their health insurance.

For about three years after George died, I participated in an informal group of twenty families in Lexington who had been working together to plan supported housing for their young adult children with disabilities. About half of the young adults had mental health issues, and the other half were developmentally disabled. All these young people had received adequate educational opportunities and strong family support, and all of them functioned with some degree of independence, some more than others of course. In general, those with mental health problems were much more independent than those with developmental disabilities, but they did need regular monitoring, especially around their medications.

A few of the original committee members bought into a condominium arrangement in the town of Brookline where their adult children had access to public transportation and, presumably, more employment possibilities. When Mary Ann and I visited one of these houses, she reacted warmly but I had misgivings. As time went on, I became more determined to try to find supported housing for her in Lexington, where she grew up, where she knew lots of people, and equally important, lots of people knew her.

For the first two years, all of us on the committee were very discouraged. One after another, local legislators and town officials would come meet with our committee, usually to tell us that it would be a very long time before the state would provide any services for our adult children, that they were all way down on the waiting list, and that the first to be served would be those in crisis and those with the most severe disabilities.

Then suddenly, at one meeting in 1991, we learned that a large house on the main street was to be set up as transitional living for young people with mental health issues. This house would include twelve residents and at least three would be from Lexington families. While not ideal in every way, this was still a huge step forward. Several of our committee members succeeded in placing their children there, and others managed to find suitable apartments, one in Lexington and one in neighboring Concord.

A few months after that, some of us noticed a new house being constructed by students from Minuteman Regional vocational high school; this house was just two blocks from the center of town. As we investigated, we discovered the house would have four bedrooms and two complete baths. Then we learned this house was owned by the town of Lexington as part of its affordable housing, which meant the rent would be approximately half of the going market rate. Four of us from the committee who had daughters with varying developmental disabilities launched a campaign to secure this house for our four daughters. We worked hard and put together an application to Lex-Hab, the agency that manages Lexington's affordable housing. We spoke before the appropriate housing committee and also with our own individually elected town officials.

Our efforts paid off and we did, in fact, secure the house. At that point we had to decide how we would operate it—who would hire staff, who would supervise them, who would determine hours, and so forth. We quickly decided to engage one of the disability housing vendors in the area, as they have knowledge and experience. We interviewed representatives from several vendors before making a decision we all agreed on.

After a few years we switched to another vendor, but all in all the house has run smoothly. One by one, little by little, the other families have relocated and moved their daughters to their new family locations, many miles from Lexington. At this writing, Mary Ann is the last of the original occupants, but it would be very difficult to get her to move.

Our daughters were not eligible for state support because they were not severely enough disabled and still had family homes where they could live. Therefore we had to figure out how to pay for the house on our own. Since George had died, Mary Ann was receiving Social Security Survivors Benefits (SSSB) rather than SSI (Supplemental Security Income). SSI is funded by general tax revenues, not by Social Security taxes. Her SSSB monthly benefit was about twice what her SSI had been. Without her SSSB, she and I could not possibly have afforded the cost of her house. We four families were paying all the costs, including staffing, food, rent, and utilities. Because of the financial pressures on all of us, we managed with minimum staffing, and only had about thirty hours per week with no overnight staff. On the other hand, all four of us lived right in Lexington, so we were close by in case of any emergency. In order to minimize our costs, we joined with another privately-funded house in Lexington to do some joint fundraising, and we were fortunate to have that leadership assumed by the brother of one of the women in the other house. After several years we were able to secure some funding from the state, but Mary Ann still pays 75 percent of her monthly income toward the operation of the house.

Mary Ann loves living at her Waltham Street home. Because it is so close to the center of Lexington, she has maximum independence. She walks to the bank and to choir practice and church. She also walks to the town pool and to the Fourth of July Lions Club carnival. She goes independently to the annual Patriots Day parade, which celebrates the Battle of Lexington and Concord, the start of the American Revolution in 1775. Occasionally she walks to the high school track to walk for exercise.

Shortly after Mary Ann moved into her new home, a caseworker from the Department of Mental Retardation came to visit her and do an assessment of her needs. At one point she handed Mary Ann a mirror and asked her, "What do you see?" Mary Ann responded happily, "It's beautiful!" I was ecstatic—she had spent so many years living with very low self-esteem, the result of constantly being corrected, and hardly ever doing anything "right." Everyone around her, teachers and family members, were well intentioned in trying to teach her appropriate language and behavior, but our actions must have chipped away at her self-confidence.

Final confirmation that I had made the right decision about Mary Ann's housing came on the Sunday afternoon of the first Thanksgiving weekend after she moved in. As I drove her back from my house to her house, she suddenly said, "Mom, I've had enough of you!" She said this not in anger or even defiance, but as a clear statement of independence. It was wonderful to hear this exclamation from my twenty-seven-year-old daughter.

At one point I became acquainted with a family whose daughter with autism was also twenty-seven and living in a house similar to Mary Ann's, but the residents have greater needs—they require much more staffing, including overnight staff. The families are paying all the costs, but as the parents approach retirement age, they must turn to the state for help. This particular young woman, at some point in her school years, was given an inflated IQ score of ninety-four, which was not accurate then and certainly is not applicable now. However, that score is part of her permanent record and is being used to disqualify her from receiving services from the Massachusetts Department of Mental Retardation,[24] the only available source of residential help for adults with autism in the state. Eventually I learned that this family, and the others in that house, did succeed in getting help from the state, but it took a couple of years of intense effort.

The economic crash of 2008–09 has brought more families to this crisis. Nearly every week I hear from another family with an autistic adult who is being denied state services because he or she has "passed" the IQ test. Sometimes these are people who are clearly more disabled than Mary Ann. This is one more example of the unresolved challenges that still face adults with disabilities once they leave school.

Food note: Unfortunately most of the personnel who staff Mary Ann's house are not very adventurous about food. And one resident did not like any fish or seafood. However, Mary Ann is not easily denied when it comes to food. One staff person told me that Mary Ann would regularly eat a can of sardines at dinner. This seemed perfectly fine. However, one day when I was visiting the house, I checked the cupboard and to my utter amazement I discovered that Mary Ann was eating not the little three-ounce can, but a three-*pound* can of sardines, all at one meal. Consumption of the omega-three acids was fine, but this was overkill. I worked with the house staff director and persuaded Mary Ann instead to take one of the small, three-ounce cans of sardines for lunch two or three times a week.

---

24 This department has recently changed its name to Department of Developmental Services, a major step forward. The new name identifies the services, not the clients, and it has gotten rid of the term "mental retardation."

CHAPTER 9
Protection Temporarily Forgotten: Disaster

On a cold, snowy Monday morning in January 1994, I received a call from Mary Ann's vocational program. The caller told me Mary Ann's hand was badly swollen, so much so that she could not put on her glove. I dropped what I was doing at work in Boston and picked her up at her work to take her to our family physician. As she approached the car, I noticed she was not walking normally, that something was wrong there too, in addition to her swollen hand. It took lengthy, careful questioning before I, her residential staff person, and the doctor elicited from her what had happened. Jay, a young man who had started spending time with her, had taken her to his home in Burlington, a neighboring town, on Sunday afternoon. We think he had begun preliminary sexual advances when Mary Ann suddenly objected and asked to go home, saying it was suppertime. (I later concluded her autism had saved her from rape—it was 6:00, suppertime, and you do not mess with the regular schedule of Mary Ann's meals.)

By the middle of the week, Karen Morgan, the staff person, with my permission and Mary Ann's agreement, did a thorough examination of her body and discovered horrendous bruises on her trunk, primarily her back, including one large bruise that was the print of a boot. Karen had the good sense to take Polaroid pictures of the bruises immediately. We then learned that as Mary Ann moved to Jay's car in order to go home, he had knocked her down in the snow and then kicked her several times. At that point I got on the phone, seeking information and advice from many sources. Ultimately I contacted the District Attorney's office, the Disabled Persons Protection Commission (DPPC), and the local Burlington police department. Both the DA's office and the local police were very, very responsive and helpful. The

DPPC conducted an investigation but they were not as thorough or as helpful as the other two agencies.

The DA conducted an investigation and filed charges against Jay, and advised Mary Ann and me to get a restraining order against him. Thus began a lengthy, but ultimately successful, journey with law enforcement that involved close cooperation among the local police from three neighboring towns, the DA staff, victim witness advocates, and Mary Ann and me.

Because of Mary Ann's disability, she was required to undergo a competency hearing. Presumably, this action was required so that her report of the incident could be trusted and she could competently respond to questions. Her counselor, Dr. Condon, and I did what we could to prepare her for that experience. At the end of the hearing, which occurred on a Monday morning, the judge turned to her and asked, "Mary Ann, do you have any questions?" and she said to the judge, "Did you go to church yesterday?" After that, he could hardly declare her incompetent.

I later learned that within five minutes of Mary Ann's question to the judge, word had spread throughout the very large, multi-floored Middlesex County Courthouse.

We then proceeded to a jury trial at the same courthouse in Cambridge where Jay had been indicted for his attack on Mary Ann. Because Mary Ann and I appeared as witnesses, we were not allowed to attend the trial until the decision was announced, five days later. By that point, Mary Ann was ready to return to work rather than sit around at the courthouse. After the guilty verdict was announced and a decision was made to send Jay to a state correctional facility, I went to Mary Ann's house to wait for the van to arrive from her work. As she emerged from the vehicle I told her the news that Jay would be going to jail, and she literally jumped up and down with exuberant joy. This was one of those times when her autism melted away, and she reacted exactly as anyone else in her place would.

In the final chapter of this episode, we were advised to take out a permanent restraining order against Jay. On Wednesday, May 15, 1996, Mary Ann and I went to Concord District Court at 8:50 AM to await our call to the hearing room. About 9:30, Jay showed up, soon followed by his parents, but no lawyer.

Mary Ann was tense and quiet. The victim witness advocate was not present this day, as she was at another court hearing.

Following is the content of the hearing:

Jay: Your honor, I just want closure on this incident. I have served my time in prison, and I want to move on.

Judge McGill (to Mary Ann): Tell me what happened on that day (Jan. 16, 1994).

Mary Ann started to read from her affidavit, but I told her the judge just wanted her to tell him. She said: Jay pushed me down in the snow and kicked me.

Judge McGill: Why did he do that?

Mary Ann: Because I was bad?

Judge McGill: No, Mary Ann, you were not bad.

Jay: I do not intend to have any contact with Mary Ann.

Judge McGill: That's good, because that is exactly what I am going to order.

That final response from Mary Ann hurt me the most in all that had happened. That evening I asked Fred to go with me, and we went to Mary Ann's house to talk to her. I suggested that she go upstairs and bring down Judge Teddy, a Vermont teddy bear wearing a judge's gown that I got her after the trial. As we sat in the living room, Fred and I assured Mary Ann that she was not bad—that she was not the bad one when Jay hurt her, but he was, and that she was not a bad person. Then I role-played with Judge Teddy, telling her that the bear was Judge McGill and Judge Brant, and Judge Teddy told her that she was not bad, Jay was.

As I role-played the judge, Mary Ann smiled broadly and when I finished, she said "Just like the Brady Bunch." When I asked her if there was a judge on the Brady Bunch, she just said yes.

I told her she should look at Judge Teddy and be reminded that she's not a bad person, she's a good person. That Judge McGill and Judge Brant said so.

I do feel I share some responsibility for this sad development in Mary Ann's life. I have always wanted her life to be as "normal" as realistically possible, living and working in the community. However, that particular time I slipped and unwittingly sacrificed a level of protection for her. When Jay had come to my home on Christmas Eve, wanting to spend time with Mary Ann, it did not occur to me that he had any but the best intentions. After all, he drove a van for Mary Ann's vocational program—surely he would not do something that would jeopardize his job. How wrong I was. It did not occur to me that Jay's intentions toward Mary Ann and her friends were the very reason he had sought this job. Fred had doubts from the beginning and I should have listened to him. Clearly, had George still been alive, he almost certainly would have set me straight.

We think Jay probably has a disability far worse than that of Mary Ann or her friends and housemates. This was one of those rare times, though, when I could not pitch in to help Jay or his parents. My own dear daughter had to come first.

CHAPTER 10

Growing Independence and Continued Learning

*Mary Ann visiting her mother Martha at
Thanksgiving in Harrisburg, Pennsylvania*

In her late twenties and early thirties, Mary Ann had to learn how to live with three other women with disabilities and at the same time to interact with people at work and in the community who are not disabled. Throughout her life, she has confronted this duality, though she may not perceive it that way at all. She has several good friends with disabilities, one with autism, one with cerebral palsy, and one with spina bifida. She does not see them often, but she cares very much about them. She remembers their birthdays and loves to go to their birthday parties every year.

One interesting development for Mary Ann after she moved out on her own has been her increasing use of the telephone. Over the years at home, she rarely made a call, but once in her own house, she learned fairly quickly to call me, leaving a brief message on my voice mail if I was unavailable. Retaining her echolalia, she still regularly says "This is Mary Ann Ziegler. I live at 165 Waltham Street. My number is 863-2303." She always says this in the exact same rhythm and tone of voice and never gives any additional information. She says it so fast that anyone not familiar with her would have trouble understanding much of it. Now that I have a cell phone, she calls me anywhere, anytime, a fact that is both encouraging and sometimes frustrating. One time she called me right after I had boarded a plane in Columbia, South Carolina. She could not understand why I was legally required to hang up. Of course, I should have turned off the cell phone before I boarded, but I was still learning some of the fine points about cell phone usage. She is always impatient with me when I insist on ending a call, for whatever reason, whether on a cell phone or a traditional phone.

Some years ago I realized that telephone calling is much like handling money—both are basically abstract activities. Bills and coins are symbols, not objects to be purchased or exchanged. Similarly, a voice on the phone is abstract—you cannot see the person at the other end, or their location or surroundings. Autism requires concreteness and such abstract activities can be very difficult to learn.

Eventually Mary Ann even made occasional long-distance calls to her aunts and cousins in other parts of the country. This action occurred after I had tried for several years to persuade her to do it.

Some of that resistance continues. Occasionally when I call her she will say, "Why are you calling me?" Once I give her a reason she is fine, unless she is watching a football game, and then I am given short shrift.

Recently Mary Ann has shifted from saying to me, "I love you," to saying, "I like you." I have not yet figured out the significance of this change. She usually says it out of the blue, for no obvious reason. Occasionally it appears to be an effort to compensate for an error she has committed, such as continuing to perseverate when I have firmly asked her to stop.

Another interesting development is her growing interest in meeting others. A few years ago, Mary Ann was working at a Joyce Chen warehouse that distributed Chinese cooking utensils. With some other people, she packaged the utensils for shipping. In one corner of the warehouse, there was a glassed-in section for office workers. After a few months at the warehouse, Mary Ann said to her job coach, "Who are those people? I haven't met them."[25] With encouragement from her job coach, she went in and introduced herself to each of them, asking about their birthdays and, to their great amazement, telling each one the day of the week on which they were born. The glass-enclosed workers were pleased and suddenly the workers with disabilities were truly included as part of the work force.

That conversation was far from unusual. Whenever Mary Ann is introduced to someone new to her, she begins the conversation by asking the person the date and year of the person's birth. She then quickly tells the person which day of the week the person was born on. Experts consider this a savant characteristic. Mary Ann considers it a fun game. Not everyone, of course, is pleased with her question about year of birth, although most people relax once they realize Mary Ann could care less about their age.

Also interesting was her reaction to Dr. Condon's retirement. He eventually felt it was time to retire from counseling. He, of course, told Mary Ann and me in advance when the final session would occur. At this point, completely on her own initiative, Mary Ann invited him to join us for a farewell luncheon, to which he graciously agreed. She then suggested to me that we give him a farewell gift. She decided to give him a sweater, which she and I chose together.

I never knew for sure what Dr. Condon thought about all this, but I was very proud of Mary Ann. Such attachment and gestures of appreciation are not supposed to occur with autistic people.

Mary Ann can sometimes misunderstand language in dramatic ways that people around her do not recognize. One Sunday in February, we had been at Jessica Vohs' birthday party. As we were leaving, Mary Ann suddenly said with great intensity, to Jessica's mother Janet, "Theresa died in February. This is Black History Month." I had other

---

25   "Job coach" is the term used for trained staff that either introduce a person with a developmental disability to a new job or continue to support a group of such people who are working at a particular job site.

things on my mind and did not pick up on this comment until Janet reminded me of it the next day. I asked Mary Ann, "Do you think African American people always die during Black History Month?"

"Yes," she replied.

I explained to her that that was not true, that Black people die every month of the year, not just during February—Black History Month. (Theresa, who was African American, had worked at Mary Ann's group home and she had died during February a couple of years previously.)

When Mary Ann makes errors like this, it is difficult to determine to what extent her disability—her reliance on the concrete, narrow meanings of words—is responsible and how much is due to her segregated education with its separation from the usual elementary grade curriculum. Very likely, both contribute.

This is a good example of the distorted notions of cause and effect that Dr. Condon continually worked to uncover. Because she expresses these notions in personal metaphors in apparently meaningless language, they can be very difficult to translate and correct. On the other hand, just how strange is it to confuse coincidence with cause and effect? How many apparently normal people choose family birthdays as the likeliest winning numbers to play in a lottery? Why do hotels and other high buildings often omit a thirteenth floor? Furthermore, Josh Tenenbaum, a cognitive scientist at the Massachusetts Institute of Technology, maintains that the effort to identify patterns from coincidence is crucial for human learning and scientific development.[26]

Mary Ann presented an example of metaphorical language in February 1998, near the end of an ISP (Individual Service Plan) meeting. She said, "I miss overnight staff" in a wistful, longing voice. She had made this comment to me several times in recent months and I just had not gotten it. That day it suddenly hit me. I asked her, "Are your housemates bothering you?" and she said "Yes." I then asked her, "Do they bother you after the staff leaves?" and she answered "Yes." (A staff person is at her house from 4:00 PM to 8:00 PM each week day.) Unfortunately, there had been an intermittent history of Mary Ann being scapegoated by the other women in her house. Of course, it is very difficult for them to understand her disability. Additionally, because of

---

26   Joshua Tenenbaum is the Paul E. Newton Career Development Professor of Cognitive Science and Computation in the Department of Brain and Cognitive Sciences at MIT.

her autism, she is not likely to report the problem, at least not directly or in language the listener can understand.

This very important interchange is a prime example of what I call Mary Ann's private metaphors, and what Dr. Condon described more directly as her difficulty in stating a concern in words that we can understand. This difficulty with language goes to the heart of autism. It is my fervent hope that, today and tomorrow, young children with autism will have opportunities that were not available to Mary Ann. As the research explodes and we learn more about what exactly goes on within these brains, teachers and therapists should be developing greatly improved methods for teaching language and communication.

The most dramatic of Mary Ann's metaphors is the town clock in the square in Greencastle, the little town in Pennsylvania where George grew up, and where she regularly visited her Grandpa and Grandma Ziegler. An antique clock with wooden works that is located in a tower atop a bank in the square, it strikes the hour and can be heard clearly for a block or so in each direction, including the Ziegler family home a block up the street. All the Ziegler grandchildren loved the town clock when they were young, but none of the others was quite so drawn to it as a family symbol as Mary Ann was, and continues to be. Mary Ann's cousin, Helen, has suggested that perhaps the absolute regularity, correctness, and predictability of the clock add to its attraction for Mary Ann.

Mary Ann's Grandmother Ziegler died first, in August 1983, and her Grandfather Ziegler went the following February. After her grandfather's funeral, as we sat in the living room of the empty house, Mary Ann commented, "There's nothing left but the town clock." Since then, the town clock has been a powerful symbol of death for her.

As I have had time to think about Helen's suggestion of a secondary meaning for the town clock, I agree with her. For Mary Ann, hearing the clock in Greencastle reinforced her reliable, regular connection to her Ziegler relatives, including her father. Furthermore, the recurrence of death anniversaries, like birthdays, is always the same—reliably predictable like the clock.

At one point in my career, I was spending so much time in Washington, DC in connection with my work that one day I made the offhand remark, "Washington is my second home." Not long after that, Mary Ann became more than usually anxious. Eventually she began to ask when I, or we, would be moving. It took Dr. Condon and me several counseling sessions before we finally figured out that Mary Ann had misinterpreted that remark. She thought I meant that I would literally move from Lexington to Washington and she was very upset about it. It was not clear whether she feared that I would abandon her or whether she dreaded a move by the whole family. After all, we had moved several times before we settled in Lexington. Once Dr. Condon explained to her the meaning of the phrase "second home" in the context of my remark, she relaxed and stopped worrying.

Dr. Condon believed, and I agree with him, that this kind of misunderstanding of the meaning of words is a major cause of anxiety and worry for Mary Ann and also for most people with autism. It may also contribute to their devotion to sameness—once they have figured out the meaning of a situation they cannot afford to risk any change.

CHAPTER 11

More Lessons in Protection

Only a year or so after George died, Mary Ann experienced her first and only *grand mal* seizure. It occurred on a Friday at her vocational program and I was on a plane to Puerto Rico to give two speeches at the annual conference of APNI, the parent center in San Juan. Unbeknownst to me (this was before cell phones), my friend and colleague Evelyn Hausslein took Mary Ann to the doctor and Fred came home from work at noon to be with her. Once I arrived in San Juan and received this information, I confronted a tough decision: Should I stay and meet my responsibilities at the conference or immediately return home?

Perhaps it was the teacher in me, but I decided to take advantage of this situation as a learning opportunity for Fred and Mary Ann. They both needed to learn that Fred could also take care of Mary Ann in an emergency. I did cut out the extra vacation days that I had looked forward to spending with my dear friend Carmen Selles de Villa, founder and director of APNI. I gave the two speeches as planned on Saturday and then returned to Lexington on Sunday. As I hoped, Fred and Mary Ann managed very nicely during my brief absence.

This was also an important lesson for me. It had never been easy for me to ask for help or to rely on someone else, other than George, for assistance in caring for Mary Ann. I have never explored the psychology at work here. After George died, I really had no choice. Because my nationwide work often required me to travel, I made arrangements with my neighbors, John Pfeil and his wife Davy, who were retired. They very graciously agreed to be on call should Mary Ann need any assistance while I was away. It had taken me many years to accept the fact that others could help—even deserved a chance to help.

The seizure launched Mary Ann on a new series of medical tests and, ultimately, regular visits to Dr. Russell Butler, a neurologist who also specializes in autism. In no time, he and his colleagues confirmed what Dr. Huttenlocher, the neurologist at Yale, had suspected those many years earlier—Mary Ann did indeed have neurofibromatosis (NF) along with her autism. Fortunately, with medication and with regular, careful monitoring by Dr. Butler, she has had no more seizures. We assume the NF caused, or at least contributed to, the autism. Dr. Butler recently informed me that for many years, neurologists have known there is a connection between NF and autism, as well as tuberous sclerosis and autism.

Neurofibromatosis, also known as Von Recklinghausen's disease, is a genetic disorder in which tumors are formed on nerve tissue. Mary Ann's most obvious symptom is a familiar pattern of brown spots on her torso and a few on her face and legs. In addition, the tumors may cause bumps under the skin, skeletal problems, pressure on spinal nerve roots, and other neurological problems. Luckily, Mary Ann's NF is a mild form of the disorder.

After confirmation of the NF, we then engaged in comprehensive genetic counseling, including discussions with extended family members, and found no history of NF anywhere on either side of the family. We concluded the NF must have been a mutation. So far, not enough research has been done around the many cases of co-morbidity in autism. However, when I recently took Mary Ann for her periodic follow up at the NF clinic, I was pleased to learn that the director there is conducting research on autism/NF co-morbidity. He immediately included Mary Ann in his study.

Approximately 20 to 30 percent of people with autism also have a seizure disorder—one that often does not appear until adolescence or early adulthood. I have two good friends whose autistic sons died from seizures in early adulthood.

The very first time I traveled after George's death, before Mary Ann's seizure, I attended a conference in Washington, DC. I had asked the Pfeils to be on call if Mary Ann needed them, and of course I explained to her that she should call them if needed. She was still not comfortable using the telephone. Nevertheless, one evening while I was attending a reception in the conference hotel, I was called to the phone and there was Mary Ann, telling me about a power failure.

I immediately called Davy Pfeil who went next door and spent an hour with Mary Ann until the power came back on. I have since learned that fear of power failures is frequent among autistic people. One time when Mary Ann participated with a panel of autistic young adults at a conference, when she mentioned this fear, the daughter of Clara Parks, author of *The Siege,* and others on the panel nodded vigorously in agreement. My friends and I think the big problem with power failures is the suddenness, surprise, and the uncertainty of the length of time—all conditions that are very difficult for autistic people.

One thing is certain, Mary Ann wants to learn, and that drive has been apparent from the time she had enough language to express it. It was her idea to learn Spanish, starting in junior high school, and in high school it was she who wanted to take a science course. She did finally get to take biology and did remarkably well.

Starting in her late teenage years and continuing to the present, Mary Ann has been willing to speak to groups, after very careful preparation of course. Usually she and I do this together. Several times, she has appeared with me before a class taught by Professor Tom Hehir at the Harvard Graduate School of Education, and occasionally she and I do presentations as part of professional development for public school teachers and administrators. The Harvard students have always responded with great appreciation—clearly they learn a lot from a real live person with autism, just as I have learned so much from Mary Ann.

Following is a short speech that Mary Ann gave at the annual conference of the President's Committee on Employment of the Handicapped (later renamed the President's Committee on Employment of People with Disabilities) in Washington, DC.

My name is Mary Ann Ziegler. I live in Lexington, Massachusetts. I am a person with autism. I go to a vocational education program, called LABB, at Lexington High School.

I do volunteer work in the school nurse's office. I clean the tables, clean the beds, and clean the desks. Sometimes I use magic markers to make pictures to brighten the walls in the nurse's office. I go there during one period every Wednesday.

Also, I go to work at Honeywell Company in Lawrence, Massachusetts, on Tuesdays, Thursdays, and Fridays as part of my

LABB program. Once a month, I get a paycheck for my work at Honeywell. I have to wear a badge in order to go to Honeywell.

At Honeywell, I do some cutting, stripping, fast ons, ring tongs, and pin connectors. These are parts of making computers. I eat lunch in the company cafeteria. I travel back and forth to Honeywell on a special LABB bus.

I like to speak Spanish. *Yo me gusta hablar Espanol.* I hope to use Spanish in my work.

I would like to become a typist. I typed this speech on our computer. My brother lost the computer tape, so we couldn't use the printer.

I don't like getting fired. In order not to be fired, I will try not to repeat the same thing over again, like "I like to sit on the seat on the merry-go-round." My teacher gets mad and tells me that if I repeat all the time I will be fired.

I don't like to make mistakes.

I hope to have a job just like my mother and father do. I would be a good worker because I have to work hard and get to work on time. I am learning not to interrupt the other workers. I like to learn new things on the job.

For fun, I take art, sing in the chorus, and speak Spanish. I wish my mother would get tickets for the Celtics and Red Sox. When I have a job and my own apartment, I hope I can still do these things too.

I often recall my friend June's comment that living with autism "must be existential." That observation has often helped me view the world from Mary Ann's point of view. The fact that I too tend to live in an eternal present no doubt also helps.

At some point, one of Mary Ann's teachers suggested that I imitate my daughter's behavior in order to teach her. That has often been an effective device. Mary Ann usually responds with humor and insight.

I have, of course, learned a lot from Mary Ann's doctors and I suspect some of them have learned a lot from her; perhaps they have learned from me too. She contracted chicken pox in her thirties. At that time, Dr. Santis observed that whether in institutions or at home with family, people like Mary Ann probably contracted what we think of as childhood infectious diseases as adults, and these diseases may not have been accurately diagnosed or simply have had more serious consequences, which can happen with chicken pox when it occurs in adulthood. In addition to the small, segregated classes she was in until junior high school, I remembered that she <u>never</u> rode the big yellow school bus, even after she was integrated. She either went to school on a little special bus or walked.

Perhaps more important is the comment by her neurologist, Dr. Russell Butler: "We are not accustomed to seeing people like Mary Ann because they did not used to live this long." I was a little puzzled by this comment until a friend mentioned that people like her would have been living, pretty much neglected, in institutions.

Plenty of times Mary Ann has amazed me, taking me by surprise. One time when we were visiting my mother in Indiana, my aunt and uncle came by for lemonade and cookies. As we all sat around the table, suddenly Mary Ann bowed her head and said grace, a standard prayer before a meal. We had no such habit at our house in Lexington; I still do not know where she learned it. My mother was pleased, but I could not very well say, "Oh, I did not teach her to do that."

On an August evening in the year 2000, Mary Ann volunteered to me the information that she had called her Aunt Mary, long distance, in Champagne, Illinois. I had not suggested that she do this, she had initiated the call—a goal that I have intermittently worked on for several years. In the past, she has sometimes made such calls to her relatives, but she has not reported to me. I consider this action another indication of major progress and learning—mature social interaction with her aunt, and the realization that I would not know she had made the call unless she told me. Finally, this episode blows me away once more with its indication that Mary Ann never stops learning and growing.

In the fall of 2000, the federal Office of Special Education Programs (OSEP) invited me to participate in a technical assistance workshop on autism in Ireland. I agreed to do it provided that Mary Ann could come too. She knows more about autism than I do and I felt strongly that her overall progress demonstrates much of the possible achievement for someone with classical Kanner autism. The staff at OSEP agreed, but then I faced a major hitch—Mary Ann did not want to go because the trip was planned for the week before Halloween and she feared she would not get back home in time for the holiday.

After much unsuccessful arguing with her, I finally faced reality and bribed her. I told her that if she went with me to Ireland, I would make sure she had *two* pumpkins to carve. That did it and she capitulated. Our friend, Gunnar Dybwad, even had a spare pumpkin that he gave to Mary Ann. She did indeed accompany me to Ireland and, of course, she had a wonderful time.

On October 24, at the Gresham Hotel in Dublin, we gathered with our group for dinner. Mary Ann talked to the other travelers—total strangers to her. Suddenly she began to talk about the town clock in Greencastle. I was puzzled, unable to identify a context for these observations. Eventually I realized that this was October 24, the date on which George had died in 1988, twelve years earlier.

After we returned home, in the early weeks in November, there was more such talk, especially during the days before and immediately following Thanksgiving. I eventually figured out that Thanksgiving brought up thoughts about her father and her Ziegler grandparents, with whom we usually spent Thanksgiving. During that time, she also expressed worry about the possibility of death for an old friend, Betsy Britten Nilson, who lived in California. I am beginning to think that "death" and "cemeteries" are metaphors for loss and for longing for friends far away. From time to time, Mary Ann asks similar questions about our friend Carmen Selles, who lived in San Juan, Puerto Rico, and about another old friend, Charlotte des Jardins, who still lives in Chicago. All three are people whom Mary Ann would see very rarely, maybe once in ten years.

Following is a message I emailed to my friend Betsy not too long ago:

I THINK I have figured out some of Mary Ann's concerns; it's probably not all that hard for someone with some brains. I think her talk about death is a metaphor for loss of people she loves, which is obvious, but also for distance, both in space and in time, again for people she loves. I think it was probably very good for her to talk to you yesterday, and to hear your voice. She was in a happy, relaxed mood at dinner last night and again today. Autism is such an incredible combination of existentialism, poetry, and sheer brain science.

Then all the questions about Liz (Betsy's daughter) and having children, I think, are about "completing the set," an autistic requirement.

Karen and Kathy (Liz's sisters) each have two children, a boy and a girl, so Liz also must have two children, a boy and a girl.

On the afternoon of April 14, 2001, Mary Ann had a phone conversation with a new friend, the son of a friend and colleague of mine, who happened to live in Durham, North Carolina. Mary Ann had never met Brandon, and had never talked to him before. They had a brief, nice, appropriate conversation, about the weather and Easter. At one point Mary Ann asked, "Do you live in Cambridge?" After his reply, she said "That's a long flight." This is another example of her personal metaphor, used here totally appropriately and understandable to anyone else—"long flight" instead of "long distance" or "far away." (But a psychologist giving her an IQ test would probably score her lower for that.)

On Sunday, February 26, 2001, Mary Ann voluntarily stayed home from church because of bad weather, snow, sleet, and ice. Until October of 2000, when she went with me to Ireland, missing two successive Sundays at church, she absolutely would *not* miss singing in the choir on Sundays. That November she missed twice because of illness, but it was almost as if a spell were broken; now, suddenly, she could think about going, whether or not it was a good idea. When she called me that February morning, as I had asked her to do, she said "Church is cancelled." When I asked her if someone had called, she replied "No, but I'm not going."

Mary Ann is apologetic about her continuing difficulty with perseveration, often repeating whole sentences. For example, during the month of October, she will demand to know exactly what date we will buy a pumpkin to carve for Halloween. Then she will demand a date for the actual carving. Long ago I learned that supplying these dates is much more important than actually sticking to them. Once she has these dates selected, she will incessantly repeat, verbatim, "I will buy the pumpkin on the twenty-fourth and I will carve the pumpkin on the twenty-eighth."

Psychologists have taught us to apply the term "perseveration" to this behavior. But it occurs to me, is it perseveration when Edgar Allen Poe repeats the word "nevermore" at the end of each verse of his poem, "The Raven"? Is it perseveration when almost every hymn and many other songs, popular, classical, folk, repeat a whole refrain after each verse? Mary Ann loves to sing "The Twelve Days of Christmas" (especially the humorous *Sesame Street* version), as it is the kind of song that takes repetition to the limit.

Instead of trying to get Mary Ann to eliminate this "inappropriate" behavior, perhaps we should help her understand it as an essential, poetic part of her being. Halloween and the pumpkin are highlights of Mary Ann's year and we should learn to support her enthusiasm, not squelch it.

In the summer of 2001, after Fred had lived with me for ten of his adult years—first for a few months in Lexington and then for nine years in my condominium in Cambridge—I decided that the situation was not so good for him. Housing costs in Cambridge and everywhere in the Boston area were so high that I knew there was no way Fred could afford a decent place of his own. After careful thought, he and I decided that I would sell my condo and the two of us would jointly purchase a multi-unit house. Hoping for a duplex, we ended up with a triple decker in Somerville, where I lived in an apartment on the first floor, Fred on the third floor, and two lovely ladies rented the second floor.

When we began this search, I asked Mary Ann if she would like to move with us, into her own apartment. She declined, preferring to stay in her house with her housemates in Lexington. One day, as Fred and I were nearing the final stages of our move, Mary Ann was with me in the car in Lexington. Suddenly she turned to me and asked, "When are we moving to Somerville?" Once I got over the shock, I asked her, "Do you want to move to Somerville?" She then replied firmly, "No thanks."

I concluded there were two possible explanations for this exchange. She may have thought that I would force her to move with us, regardless of her wishes. Perhaps she was saying what she thought I wanted to hear. In any case, she is happily continuing to live in Lexington, only two blocks from the center of town. That same year she chose to have her birthday party (December 29) at her house, not at my place or at a restaurant. Celebrating her thirty-eighth birthday at *her* house seemed to confirm her personal choice of residence and her overall independence.

People with autism are not expected to enjoy social relationships— how wrong! Because the van broke down, Mary Ann once missed the annual CMARC Open House. CMARC (Central Middlesex

Association for Retarded Citizens) is the vendor that operates Mary Ann's supported employment program and also oversees staffing at the house where she lives. Missing the open house was a huge disaster for her—she looks forward to it for a full year, and she enjoys it immensely. It involves two hundred people milling around, eating and drinking and talking. She loves it. Obviously she enjoys the eating, but she also enjoys the socializing—seeing people whom she occasionally works with and parents of her friends.

It may symbolize to her some kind of core importance of her work life—the camaraderie of it. This annual experience she has is just so different from what people with autism are expected to feel and do.

I have observed similar, surprising behavior in Mary Ann's friend David, who also works at CMARC and lives in her same neighborhood. I saw David, who is also autistic, at the wake for Jill, a woman who lived in his house. (Jill, who had Down syndrome, died quite suddenly after a series of strokes.) When I entered the room where Jill's wake was being held, I saw David at the casket, kneeling over Jill and talking softly but intently to her. Half an hour later, as I was leaving, I saw David across the room holding a framed picture of Jill and again looking at it intently. Clearly, David was experiencing deep, normal emotion.

One March on a Saturday, Mary Ann, her housemate Laura, and I went to lunch and then poked around at Walgreen's. Mary Ann spotted a tray designed for the Passover Seder. She immediately asked me if I would buy it for her to give to her job coach, Pam. (As usual, Mary Ann had brought no money with her, although Laura had carefully contributed to the cost of lunch.) Mary Ann knew that Pam is Jewish. A few days later, I learned that Pam had been surprised and delighted that Mary Ann had done this. It was, indeed, a lovely thing to do, but the true psychology of it was probably somewhat more complicated than it appeared.

First, Mary Ann loves holidays—often having only a meager understanding of their meaning. For instance, I do not think she has any knowledge about the meaning of Passover or the Seder, or of Easter for that matter, but she loves it when Passover coincides with Holy Week. I believe her attachment to holidays is a significant aspect of her autism—really an important coping mechanism because they are so regular and predictable.

Second, presenting a gift to Pam was a true, normal act of

generosity (she later repaid me) to someone she likes. Also, sharing a holiday enabled Mary Ann to connect with Pam in a mutuality that is not always possible for her. In a way her action had deeper, more personal meaning than the rest of us experience in gift giving. She was sharing with Pam her own, deep attachment to "holiday" as an essential component of her being. Perhaps this act of sharing around a mutual experience of "holiday" helps explain Mary Ann's love of Halloween; the part she has always enjoyed most is having trick-or-treaters come to the door and handing them candy.

Mary Ann's recent experiences in sharing, with Pam and with our friend Rob Cutler and others, indicate to me that a person with autism can probably learn, or develop, feelings of empathy. Simon Baron-Cohen, Professor of Developmental Psychopathology at the University of Cambridge in England, who developed a theory of autism as "mindblindness," might disagree, but I have lived with it.[27] Mary Ann's sense of empathy is not the result of behavior modification either. It is clearly an inner drive, much like what the rest of us experience.

---

27 Simon Baron-Cohen, *Mindblindness: An Essay on Autism and Theory of Mind*, (MIT Press, 1995).

CHAPTER 12
Some Observations about Autism Today

I continually say that Mary Ann was diagnosed with classical, Kanner autism. However, as more and more research goes on and more and more is learned about the disability, more likely disabilities, it may turn out that Kanner's description will no longer serve as the touchstone, the *sine qua non*. Certainly, more and more evidence supports a conclusion that autism falls into two distinct categories: the disability that exists from, or before, a child's birth, and the disability that strikes after fifteen or more months of normal development. There may also be a third distinct category in which autism occurs along with a second disability or disorder.

In recent years, nationally-known celebrities have been speaking out publicly about their children and grandchildren with autism. This openness has had an enormously positive effect, both on other families and on legislative and research efforts. The positive results of work by football players Doug Flutie and Dan Marino, Congressman Dan Burton, NBC President Robert Wright, talk show host Don Imus, and others have made major contributions to public understanding and increased openness about autism.

Within Massachusetts, parents and advocates have been able to beat back a disastrous proposed cut in services by the Department of Developmental Services (formerly Department of Mental Retardation) and the Department of Mental Health. Response from legislators has been very positive. I believe this response reflects a cultural shift in the last twenty-five or so years, a shift that has occurred for many reasons. But one big reason is the fact that leading, publicly visible people are so open about their family members with mental retardation, autism, and other disabilities.

77

This change has also been helped by individual heroes like the autistic high school basketball star in Greece, New York and by Dick and Rick Hoyt. The Hoyts, father and son, run in the Boston Marathon every year, with father Dick pushing son Rick in a wheelchair. Rick has severe cerebral palsy and cannot walk or speak but he graduated from Boston University and, with his computer, he often communicates a wonderful sense of humor. The Hoyts, who usually finish the race in less than three hours, have personally changed the views of thousands of runners and spectators who can no longer look down on Rick as a helpless, worthless victim.

I still have grave concerns about the temptations offered by specialized segregated schools—that is, schools dedicated to autistic children. Often these start with the most benign intentions, but eventually they resist efforts to return the children to inclusive settings in their neighborhood schools. Also, for some reason, it has been next to impossible for these specialists to provide their services within inclusive public schools. And of course, there is always the risk of ending up with cruel, horrendous institutions like so many that have made the news over the years, including an infamous one in Massachusetts. All of these operate behind a veneer of "protection" for the children.

Researchers in this country and around the world, including Matthew Belmonte, formerly at MIT then at Cambridge University in England, and now at Cornell University, are engaged in an explosion of findings about ways the autistic brain develops and works.[28] Their findings, including exciting ones about "mirror neurons," have relevance not only for the cause of autism but also for the best ways to teach our children.

We seem to be getting close to identifying the various genes that are involved, but we urgently need to identify the various environmental factors that trigger the genetic problem, such as the inability to excrete heavy metals. Even though sometimes there is a familial tendency, we must admit that most cases probably are the result of spontaneous mutation, especially cases like Mary Ann's with obvious co-morbidity.

I am reminded of the Rubella epidemic in the 1960s. It produced

---

28   Matthew Belmonte, is Assistant Professor of Human Development at Cornell, where he continues to conduct research in the neurobiology of autism, utilizing the latest developments in fMRI.

large numbers of deaf children, as well as blind children, but we tend to forget that many of the children in both of these groups were also autistic. It is also worthwhile reviewing Jane Hollenbeck's observations about the similarities in spatial awareness in both blind and autistic children.[29]

I continue to be amazed by the lack of research into the gender aspects of autism. No matter where you look in the world, regardless of race or socioeconomic status, autism occurs at a ratio of approximately four boys to one girl. Shouldn't this factor readily tell us something? For this reason, and also the variation within the disability, Mary Ann has never had any girlfriends who are much like her. I am finally beginning to see occasional references to this factor but still no definitive research.

As I have helped Mary Ann prepare to speak as part of a panel of people with autism, I have been struck by the partnership we employ. I keep recalling topics or observations that I *know* from experience are important to her. When I make suggestions to her, I can tell from her reaction whether or not I have been correct. For instance, right now she is ecstatic about her voice lessons. When I suggested that she talk about the way she loves to go on learning, even in her mid-forties, and that she enjoys learning to sing better, she responds with enthusiasm. In the past, when I have made lists of her likes and dislikes, her responses have been very clear even though she would have had difficulty initiating the lists herself.

This factor has implications for the ways we teach language to autistic children. Again, we should start *where they are*, and with topics that interest them. Our family did that when Mary Ann was very young, although we did not realize it at the time. Furthermore, as parents we do that unconsciously with all our children, beginning when they are infants. We do not, after all, begin by discussing Emanuel Kant or Shakespeare or Einstein with our newborns.

Mary Ann's reaction to my coaching for her presentations reminds me very much of the demeanor I see when our autistic friend, Rob Cutler, types a passage with the support of his facilitator. I have felt from the beginning that the major value of facilitated communication, when

---

29 The late Jane Hollenbeck was a psychologist who wrote a lengthy essay about one of her patients who was blind. She compared the spatial awareness difficulties of blind people with those who are autistic.

it is done properly with well-trained facilitators, is its recognition of the autistic person's autonomy—his/her personhood. There is no question that Rob is speaking for himself, and he has become a happier, more relaxed person since he gained access to facilitated communication. I have observed a similar phenomenon among the members of a new self-advocacy group in Pennsylvania, organized by Bill Stillman.[30]

Rob's facilitated writing is focused almost totally on advocacy now, but why wouldn't it be? He has lived for fifty years with a mother, Barbara, who has lived her entire adult life practicing and preaching advocacy on behalf of people with autism and other disabilities. Furthermore, he has learned from his mother and brother and friends the language that enables him to express the pain he has suffered while living in an institution and the frustration he endured for so long in being denied elemental personhood by almost everyone outside his family.

Certainly our autistic offspring can be expected to reflect what is going on around them, starting with the family. Mary Ann's echolalia, which I described in chapter six, often contained fragments of things she had heard in the household or on TV. Although I did not see it at the time, this ability to absorb the environment constitutes a strong indicator for the value of inclusion in regular classrooms as much as possible. Whether or not they express it in what we consider a "normal" way, our autistic children are constantly absorbing much of what goes on in their environment.

One summer, Mary Ann, Fred, and I spent a weekend at the New Hampshire summer home of Betsy and Don Anderson. The Anderson's retreat was part of a large farm and farmhouse in southwest New Hampshire. Other visitors were also there. Betsy later told me that after we went home, a gentleman with mild cerebral palsy who was also there visiting another family asked Betsy if Mary Ann had CP—he had not met her, simply observed her walking from a distance. He had seen her awkward way of walking. This gentleman's observation confirms the findings of Anne Donnellan, Martha Leary, Ralph Mauerer, and others that autism involves essential "movement differences" that we observe

---

30   William Stillman, an adult with Asperger syndrome, has published several books and most recently a column in *Huffington Post* on the Internet. He delivers many speeches and workshops and has his own Web page: www.williamstillman.com.

in autistic people. Often, they are unable to activate their muscles, especially those involved with speech, in a normal way.

Occasionally autism literally pays off. On June 21, 2002, Mary Ann received an award as Employee of the Year from her vocational program. In preparation for the event, she and I did some careful review of her clothes, hoping she would look appropriately presentable. After I found that two of her favorite dresses needed dry cleaning, we took them to the local cleaner who promised to have them ready the next day, the day before the program's open house. When we returned to pick them up, the counter clerk informed us that a machine had broken down and the dresses would not be ready until Friday—the day of the event. At that point, in her uninhibited autistic manner, Mary Ann made it very clear how frustrated she was. Though my behavior was a little more subdued, I of course was not happy either. When I stopped to pick up the two dresses on my way to Mary Ann's house to help her get ready for the party, the counter girl had them ready and then told me how sorry they all were to have disappointed Mary Ann. They were so sorry that they gave us a $20 credit toward further dry cleaning.

When I arrived at Mary Ann's house, she had already selected another dress that had not needed cleaning and she was all dressed, ready for the party.

Mary Ann is very reluctant to report pain or physical discomfort. She will remain silent even about severe pain or discomfort, like when her attacker knocked her down in the snow and then stomped on her. The same reticence is also true for her housemate, Ann Meehan, but Ann is not autistic. Is this an example of one area in which they have absolute control? Is it a statement of independence? An interesting kind of stoicism? Or does it stem from bad experiences in the past? Or are they truly not experiencing pain and discomfort as others do?

In the summer of 2005, as we were driving down Route 128 south to Nantasket Beach for what we assumed would be our last trip for the season, Mary Ann began to talk about Vermont. She mentioned a vacation stop we had enjoyed at the Equinox Hotel in Manchester, Vermont. Suddenly she asked, "Is there a Solstice Hotel?" It took me a few minutes to figure out this one, but later I discovered that when she posed the question, we were about two weeks away from the Autumn Equinox. I had to tell her I did not know of a hotel with that name. A quick search on the Internet indicated no such hotel, but did reveal several that featured special celebrations for both the Summer and the Winter Solstice, including one in Basel, Switzerland, and several in Canada.

During this Saturday drive, which happened to occur on Rosh Hashanah, Mary Ann also asked me her usual questions about religion, specifically about certain friends and their religion. "How is Phyllis Sneirson? How does she celebrate Rosh Hashanah? Do you have other Jewish friends? Do you have friends who are Jehovah's Witnesses?" After I named a couple of friends who were Jehovah's Witnesses, she named a former staff person and then she asked, "Why do Jehovah's Witnesses not celebrate holidays?"

I think all these questions, including the one about a Solstice hotel, were related; the theme is celebrating holidays. As we started out, I had suggested that the heavy traffic might be due to Rosh Hashanah observances. My assumption was Mary Ann probably thought that we should celebrate the equinoxes and the solstices—and she's right.

At times like this, Mary Ann's language conveys an almost Joycean stream of consciousness. And, again, there is an existential richness in her thinking.

The latest, very positive development in Mary Ann's life has involved taking voice lessons from Robert Gartside, a superb teacher now retired from Boston University. Bob had no experience teaching voice to people like Mary Ann, but he is one of those rare, excellent teachers. At each lesson, Mary Ann is totally engaged and usually does exactly what he tells her to do; she even asks to do the warm-up exercises. She can sometimes be too insistent about the choice of songs, but Bob has learned to be strong but gentle in persuading Mary Ann to make the appropriate choices.

On Saturday, January 25, 2003, Mary Ann and I attended one of the regular vocal concerts that Bob Gartside sponsored, which featured five of his students. At the reception after the concert, Mary Ann approached one of the singers with fairly appropriate conversation and they ended up singing "Amazing Grace" together. After Mary Ann walked away, I mentioned that she was autistic and the singer replied, "My brother is also autistic. He sings well too, but he is not as articulate as Mary Ann."

Later, after I took Mary Ann to one of her favorite restaurants and was driving her back to her house, I asked her to sing for me. Without hesitation, she sang the entire theme music for the TV program *Masterpiece Theatre*. I doubt if she ever watches that program now, and I think she must remember the music from twenty-five or thirty years ago, at a time when George and I watched it regularly. After *Masterpiece Theatre*, she then proceeded to sing theme music from one TV show after another, most of which I did not know at all. Fascinated and curious about this, when I got home I went to the WGBH-TV Web page, the channel on which *Masterpiece Theater* was shown, and submitted an inquiry about that music—I had long wondered about the source of it but never asked. In response to my inquiry, someone at WGBH-TV in Boston replied, "The Mobil *Masterpiece Theater* theme music, titled "Rondeau," was composed by J.J. Mouret (1687–1783)."

As I have reported at various points, Mary Ann's questions often are totally unexpected and often seemingly out of context or socially inappropriate. Even though her questions are sometimes not appropriate for her age, I always answer her as best I can because her education and her life experience both have been so unusual.

A few years ago, George's sister Ann experienced metastasis of the breast cancer we all thought had been cured five years before. Mary Ann was full of questions: "When will Aunt Ann die? When will we go to the funeral? How many nights will we stay in Philadelphia? Who will drive me back to Lexington?" As we drove home from Philadelphia to Lexington after the funeral she asked, "Where is Aunt Ann now?" (In heaven.) "How did she get there? (An angel came and got her and took her to heaven.) "Is Gunnar in heaven too?" (She was referring to Gunnar Dybwad, who would certainly be amused by the question.) I gave Mary Ann the answers that Dr. Condon had recommended several years earlier. He and I agreed it was important to give her answers that were consoling rather than worry about my own specific beliefs.

On the trip home from Philadelphia, we stopped at the Traveler Book Restaurant in Union, Connecticut, near the Massachusetts border on Interstate 84. This restaurant overflows with second-hand books and customers are urged to take along two or three books, free, at each visit. Mary Ann immediately spotted a row of cookbooks and chose three different microwave cookbooks, each published by a different manufacturer of microwave ovens. Later, she pulled down a book titled *Israel* and checked a vocabulary list in the back. She was pleased to find what I gather were Hebrew words for "tea" and "coffee," and then she objected that she could not find a word for "fall" or "autumn." I urged her to take the book but she insisted on putting it back on the shelf and leaving it there. Thus, I had no easy way of checking it for future reference. Her interest in print material is almost always narrow, very specific, and of course concrete. It amazes me how quickly she zeroes in on the items that interest her.

As I was unpacking after our trip to Philadelphia, I came across the notes I had made as I drove around Danbury, Connecticut, trying to find the offices of a mortgage broker that I was dealing with, hoping to refinance our mortgage before the rates soared back up. (Mary Ann and I had stopped in Danbury overnight going down and again returning in order to break up the stress of driving in the heavy traffic.) A staff person at the mortgage company responded to my cell phone inquiries and tried to direct me, but I am not accustomed to talking on the phone while driving. At one point she suggested that Mary Ann use the phone, repeating the directions to me aloud. We tried, but the young lady did not know Mary Ann or anything about her and, of course, she talked too fast.

Unpacking, I found the memo pad with our notes. After two pages full of detailed notes in my writing, I came to one page of notes that Mary Ann had written—they were perfectly fine and clear, but incomplete. I happened to drop the pad and when I looked down I saw the back of the last page which contained the large printed text, "We're Lost." During this search, which lasted only about ten minutes, hampered by large construction equipment on the street blocking our view of some of the landmarks, Mary Ann had become more and more agitated, as she always did when I make a wrong turn or become uncertain about directions. Several years ago, a staff person at her house taught her to write down her urgent concerns rather than continue to repeat them orally. As usual, this device helped the both of us, even though I did not realize at the time what she had done.

Her agitation subsided quickly once we arrived at the office destination. She responded quickly to the warm welcome of the staff and immediately engaged them in conversation.

Recently when I went to pick Mary Ann up to take her to her counseling session, I walked into a "teachable moment" going on between her and her house staff person—a wonderful young man who, at the time, had an apartment in the lower level of the house.

Mary Ann had needed information from Michael and she had gone downstairs to speak to him. She knocked on his door and he asked from within, "Who's there?" She then opened the door and said "Michael, my mother wants to talk to you."

Michael tried to explain to Mary Ann that it was not appropriate for her to open his door until or unless he told her to. She was trying to respond to his teaching, but it soon became clear to me that she did not fully understand the lesson. Finally I interceded and said to her, "Mary Ann, when you knock on Michael's door and he is on the other side and he cannot see you, he has no way of knowing it is you there. When he asks 'Who is it?' you should just say 'It's Mary Ann' and then *wait* until either he opens the door or he says 'Come in.'" She responded, "Oh, I see," and immediately she wanted to role play the episode. Thus, what looked like socially inappropriate, impolite behavior was in fact a basic autistic lack of understanding of the situation.

After this episode, Mary Ann practiced a technique Michael taught her to use when she is upset—take ten deep breaths. When I observe her doing this, I am not sure whether the deep breathing, or simply doing something for which she will get positive reinforcement, is what helps. Perhaps, the activity just takes her mind off the problem at hand. It may, of course, be all three together. In any case, it almost always helps.

On a Saturday afternoon in 2008, between Good Friday and Easter, I took Mary Ann to the local area office of the Department of Mental Retardation, which provides services for people with autism. During the following year, the name was changed to the Department of Developmental Services, part of a nationwide movement to eliminate use of the term "mentally retarded" at every level. When we arrived at the office, staff people were holding auditions for a talent show to be scheduled later in the year.

As Mary Ann and I walked in, a young man with Down syndrome was playing the piano. He played with great confidence and skill and beamed when the audience applauded him. Then Mary Ann sang two solos from *My Fair Lady*. Since we had been unable to arrange for an accompanist, she sang two songs *a capella*, with no difficulty at all.

Next came Betty, a blind woman who relied on her white cane and her attendant. This talented lady sat at the piano and played one song after another, with no written music in front of her of course. The last song Betty played was one familiar to Mary Ann and to others in the audience, all of whom sang along with her. Then it hit me, why not have Mary Ann and Betty perform together?

At that point, the two ladies delivered several songs from *The Sound of Music* together, almost as if they had rehearsed them. They were having such a good time that they would have continued for the rest of the afternoon if we had not intervened.

Betty and Mary Ann had never sung together before, much less actually rehearsed. They simply melded their talents together much as any other music-loving performers would do.

Among the many pleasures of the afternoon was the fact that the staff and caretakers in attendance expressed no great surprise at what they heard: pleasure, yes, but not surprise. They knew that these people, who in the past would have been patronized and discriminated against, actually possessed superior talents equal to only a few people without disabilities. Furthermore, they were taking the necessary steps to sponsor a talent show where these people could share their talents with a larger audience.

The afternoon ended with a rousing song by two college students who would also appear in the show. Thus this would be a true talent show and not just a disability showcase.

For me, this Saturday afternoon experience was a badly needed reminder. Thirty-five years ago such an event would have been impossible, not even dreamed of.

CHAPTER 13
Continuing to Learn from My Teacher

It gets harder, not easier, to know the best way to deal with some of Mary Ann's socially inappropriate behavior now, in her adult years. At a corn festival in a neighboring town celebrating the end of summer, Mary Ann bought her second ticket for a chicken dinner and then went immediately to the front of a long line of people waiting for the next batch off the grills. I was sitting far enough away that I could not get to her in time to send her to the back of the line, but I did, of course, scold her after she sat down. Was that the "appropriate" thing for a mother to do with a forty-year-old daughter? I'm not sure. What made it more difficult was that the people around her did not object. In fact, strangers sitting across from me thought it was admirable that the people in line had treated her kindly. In fact, she probably would not object if someone had barged ahead of her in line.

This experience took me back to Mary Ann's early years when she was so attracted to various textures, including suede, corduroy, and long hair. At that time strangers usually responded, "Oh that's all right," not realizing that their reaction simply made it harder for Mary Ann to learn appropriate behavior.

One of the more difficult aspects of parenting Mary Ann has been the fact that she has rarely volunteered information to me, including the unpleasant things that have happened to her. For instance, three years after the fact, she told me about a teacher at the special school she attended who regularly hit her fingers with a ruler. I was shocked and angry, but by then we had moved far away and the teacher had also moved to another assignment. When Mary Ann was a child, I concluded her silence regarding the matter occurred mainly because she assumed that anything she knew, I also knew. Unfortunately, she had not yet acquired enough language for me to test that hypothesis.

This characteristic creates difficulties for support staff and housemates, as well as for me. Staff members currently serving her at her vocational program, as well as her residence, are becoming more knowledgeable and more sophisticated and they have learned to communicate to me everything they think I need to know. They no longer assume that Mary Ann will tell me.

Twice in the last six years, Mary Ann has developed serious infections—one on her leg and one on her foot. As usual, she did not volunteer information to anyone, including me. Each time her staff people were observant and caught the problem, but only after it had advanced to a crisis. After these two episodes, and knowing the possibility that her NF could cause tumors, we all agreed that a staff person must regularly give her a full-body check.

During the second episode, which required several days in the hospital with the administration of three different antibiotics, one of the church choir members called me to check on Mary Ann's progress and to inquire about bringing flowers to her.

Not long ago, when Mary Ann's church choir was scheduled to sing at another joint service, her choir director, Cheryl Duerr, asked for a volunteer to sing a solo at the regular service. Unbeknownst to me or to Mary Ann's voice teacher, she volunteered. We learned later that she had delivered a lovely solo of "Pie Jesu," by Gabriel Faure. When I commented to a friend how frustrating it can be when Mary Ann withholds information from me, my friend said, "Well, why not? Anyone her age would do that. Adults don't tell their parents every last thing going on in their lives."

It is ironic that Mary Ann continues to live in her hometown, while Fred and I have moved away. For me, at least, this is the opposite from what one could expect. However, each of us, including Mary Ann, has made a personal choice which has been honored.

For a little over a year, I had the privilege of working for the Mental Health Services Program for Youth (MHSPY), a wraparound program for children with mental health issues living in five suburban towns just outside Boston. With a core staff of social workers, several parent partners serving as support and advocates for families, and headed by a committed physician, MHSPY operated a true wraparound program for low-income children with a variety of emotional and behavioral needs.

With strong commitment to the wraparound model, MHSPY relied on the strengths and talents of the children and their families. The approach was always positive, never negative or judgmental, and it operated on a team basis, with parents and other family members serving as crucial members of the team. MHSPY staff members have learned to work collaboratively with physicians, local hospitals, and school personnel, both public and private. MHSPY continues to be dedicated to supporting these children within their families and communities and, as much as possible keeping them out of long-term residential placement away from their families.

After a few months at MHSPY I began asking myself, "Why can't we have a program like this for our children on the autism spectrum?" This kind of program would have been wonderful for Mary Ann and for George and me. Eventually I discovered that such a program did in fact exist and had been operating in Pennsylvania for over ten years. That program is operated by Youth Advocate Programs Inc., an agency founded thirty years ago by pioneers in the modern methods of helping adjudicated youth and keeping them out of prisons and other institutional placements.

I learned about the Youth Advocate Autism Program when I chanced upon a job announcement in one of my email messages. As I checked it out, I was so totally amazed and thrilled to find that such a service existed that I decided to apply for the position of National Autism Coordinator myself rather than look around for other applicants. My thirty years of work with the Federation had given me contacts throughout the country, abroad, and within the federal government; I was confident this experience would help me promote expansion of the Youth Advocate Autism Program.

I did spend three years at Youth Advocate Programs working with the autism initiative and helping prepare to replicate it in other states. As always with a new program initiative, I quickly encountered funding challenges, including great variations in Medicaid coverage and also coverage by private insurers from state to state. I also have had to deal with new sets of terminology and acronyms—like TSS (therapeutic support staff) and BSC (behavioral service counselor), for instance. Nevertheless, the basic program, with its mission of building on the strengths and interests of the child and family is a sound one and Youth Advocates' rigorous outcome studies have confirmed this positive effect.

Since moving back to the Boston area from Pennsylvania, I have helped start an autism institute at Wheelock College that includes the Youth Advocate Program as a partner. A major goal of the institute is to help current and future professionals serving people with autism learn to foster respectful and inclusive relationships. We are committed to promoting the positive elements of the wraparound approach for the teachers and therapists who plan to work with children or adults on the autism spectrum.

The idea of "wraparound" services was being developed and promoted around the same time that the team approach to special education was being enshrined in law. Theoretically, the two ideas complement each other, but unfortunately, they have been implemented largely as separate, parallel efforts—one emphasizing education and the other therapy, as if these two aspects of children's lives are completely separate.

An additional, complicating challenge has arisen from the varying vocabulary used by the various professionals who work with autistic children: special educators, speech and language therapists, occupational therapists, psychologists and psychiatrists, neurologists, and of course pediatricians. Recently geneticists and neurological researchers have added their lingo. To make matters worse, the basic labels for autism have changed over time, including childhood schizophrenia, infantile autism, mental illness, atypical, and emotionally disturbed.

More and more I see confirmation of my friend June Burke's remark about Mary Ann's life experience as "existential." For example, the Danish philosopher Soren Kierkegaard (1813–1855), the "father of existentialism," said that "truth is subjectivity," that human beings can be understood only from the inside, in terms of their lived and experienced reality and dilemmas, and not from the outside, in terms of a biological, psychological, social, scientific, or other externally imposed theory of human nature. In fact, both William Stillman, author and speaker who has Asperger syndrome, and Bob Millburne, founder of the Youth Advocate autism program, as well as Donna Williams before them, use the phrase "from the inside out" as they teach new workers about the autism experience and how to understand it.

During Mary Ann's forty-six years, we have experienced a gradual but deep and irreversible change in attitudes and behavior toward people with autism. As they have gradually been included more and more in school and community, as their teachers and their classmates have eventually become their co-workers and neighbors, our people with autism are being accepted for the wonderful, fascinating, and often talented people that they are. Not long ago, I was shopping for clothes for Mary Ann in a local department store. The lady at the checkout desk was distracted, having a hard time concentrating on the purchases, and muttering "What's wrong with that boy?" I stepped out of line and went to check. Sure enough, there was a good-sized adolescent boy charging back and forth in the aisle, uttering fairly loud, unintelligible sounds. When I returned to the sales desk I said to the clerk, "He's autistic." She replied "Oh, all right," and relaxed immediately.

Such recognition and acceptance were amazing to me. In spite of the truly strange behavior, this young man was not a threat, not someone to be feared, much less someone to be escorted out of the store by local police. Just the word "autistic" was sufficient explanation.

On the other hand, some of the traditional behaviorists have not moved much. At a recent national conference on autism, Mary Ann asked a psychologist member of the Professional Advisory Board the date of her birthday, including the year. Rather than being pleased or amused, this woman scolded Mary Ann for her socially inappropriate behavior. I had a hard time controlling my indignation, but I knew that it would have no impact on that woman. Furthermore, she unwittingly revealed her own insecurity about her age of course. All Mary Ann cared about was figuring out what day of the week the woman was born on. Heaven forbid that a behaviorist should recognize an autistic person's inherent savant ability.

One big, continuing challenge comes from some of the well-intentioned service providers who keep pounding away with their insistence that autistic children must receive very intensive training as early as possible, that otherwise they will never progress as they should. This mantra does a huge disservice to the children, and perhaps even more to the parents. If the child does not "recover" from autism or at least make amazing progress toward "normalcy," the mother assumes she has failed, or has not started early enough or worked intensely enough. The parents assume the guilt for effort that is too late or inadequate. This "blame the parents" approach is not all that different from the old "refrigerator mother" blame game that was so prevalent forty years ago.

I am not quite as committed to politically correct language as some of my friends are. For instance, I am a fat lady, not a lady with fatness. I do not object to sometimes using "autistic" as an adjective because it communicates a description of characteristics, not a label for the person. And now, some of my self-advocate friends, including Temple Grandin, refer to themselves as "an autistic." (The English teacher in me cringes at this one, but I understand the philosophy at work here.) I do, however, object to the use of the term "special needs" as an adjective, for reasons of accuracy and good grammar. Furthermore, "special needs" is often used as a euphemistic adjective meaning "mentally retarded." It is interesting that people do not realize that they are giving away their unacceptable attitudes through the language they use.

For example, a flyer advertising recreation opportunities reads, "Travel and Social Programs for the special needs population." It does not call them "people," much less "people with special needs" or "with disabilities."

Here are a few more observations about language:

1. The term "mental retardation" is essentially meaningless. It has enabled people to glibly dismiss any real value of the children given that label. When I tell someone that Mary Ann is fluent, though autistic, in Spanish, often the next question put to me is, "Then she is very high functioning, not mentally retarded, right?" It is impossible to answer that question as posed. The fact is, she did excel in learning Spanish and she continually excels in singing and in her savant calendar calculations. However, at the same time she cannot handle money appropriately and she never mastered long division in spite of two fruitless years of effort by a math teacher in her vocational school.

   I am convinced the term "mentally retarded" should be discarded from our vocabulary. We have learned way too much about learning ability and the importance of individual interests, self-esteem, and expectations. I have known several young people with Down syndrome, people who have been assumed to be mentally retarded from birth, who have excelled in many ways and have eventually gone to college. Amy Robison is attending junior college and she gives speeches alongside her father Rich Robison, current executive director of the Federation for Children with Special Needs.

Any young person who cannot speak is automatically assumed to be mentally retarded—often a totally incorrect conclusion. The many non-speaking people with autism, cerebral palsy, and other physical or neurological disorders who communicate with facilitated communication or other assistive technology are helping us overcome this out-of-date idea.

2. As time goes on, I am more and more convinced that our landmark special education law in Massachusetts—known as Chapter 766 though it should be known as the Bartley-Daly Law—was absolutely correct in discarding the categorical labels and calling for the education of individual children with special needs. It would be so much better for evaluators to concentrate on the individual strengths and needs of each child—on the individual physical, neurological, and emotional needs of each child. Then teachers and parents can work together to help the child achieve his or her potential, according to the child's own strengths and interests.

Current research is showing us that autistic children confront various sensory challenges, which are not always the same for every child on the autism spectrum. It is far more important to identify each child's sensory problems rather than to come up with a label. Furthermore, do we possibly believe that children not on the spectrum never face serious sensory challenges?

Progress similar to that in education has been made in therapeutic support for children with "behavioral health needs," including those on the autism spectrum. As I indicated above, I have myself been fortunate enough to work with two of these "wraparound" programs. The autism branch of Youth Advocate Programs Inc. also serves children eligible for Pennsylvania's Medicaid services. Mainly because of Pennsylvania's distinctive Medicaid waiver, Youth Advocate's autism initiative operates with a somewhat different structure from MHSPY's, but nevertheless it does employ the wraparound model, emphasizing the strengths and interests of the child and family.

Another important innovation at Youth Advocate Programs has been the involvement of adult self-advocates in training support personnel. "Self-advocate" is the term preferred by people with autism, especially adults. Two of these self-advocates with autism make their contributions using facilitated communication.

Both of these wraparound therapeutic programs are designed around the needs of the individual child and family, and each child is approached as a child first, not as a label. The children are seen as important young people first, not as a label-driven bundle of problems that must be attacked. In this approach, both wraparound programs are similar to the Massachusetts non-categorical special education law.

Our children and families, and ultimately society, would benefit enormously if we could somehow find a way to combine the non-categorical education approach with the wraparound therapeutic approach. I know that my daughter, Mary Ann, and our family would have benefited greatly from such integration. Even now, as adults, Mary Ann and her friends would benefit from a wraparound program.

With total acceptance by immediate and extended family, a relatively good education, and a moderate amount of support as an adult, Mary Ann has been able to participate fully in life on her own terms. Not many people have tried to "cure" her or remake her in some other image, although she may not always have perceived people's efforts that way. I cannot overemphasize the importance of unconditional acceptance and love. As parents, we must always be cautious not to do things that undermine this fundamental parental approach. I am frequently reminded of the caution expressed by Ann Turnbull, co-director of the Beach Center on Disability at the University of Kansas, in many of her speeches and writings: We must avoid the "fix the broken doll" approach to our children with disabilities. Such an approach may meet the needs of caring parents, but it undermines the self-esteem of the children.

CHAPTER 14
Summary of Lessons Learned from My Teacher, Mary Ann

1. Presume intellect. Current self-advocates and professionals are absolutely correct when they insist that we "presume intellect" when dealing with anyone on the autism spectrum. But an even more important rule is, "Assume worth." For the first twelve or so years of Mary Ann's life, we had little idea of what was really going on inside that pretty head. Yet only a short time later, she mastered Spanish and high school biology and, starting in her late thirties, has become an accomplished singer.

2. Build on inherent talents and interests. Mary Ann has always flourished when she is engaging in activity that is important to her, whether singing, doing laundry, speaking Spanish to a friend, playing solitaire on the computer, watching professional football on TV, or assembling packages for shipment.

3. Be as concrete and specific as possible when talking to Mary Ann. She cannot deal with vague or approximate answers, such as "later" or "when it is over." One time when I took her to a dance concert at her high school she started to ask and repeat, "When will it end?" I was taken aback because it appeared she was thoroughly enjoying the program. After it was over, on the way home, I finally realized that she was asking this question from worry that it would end too soon; she was not asking in the ordinary sense of "I'm bored" or "I'm tired."

4. Assume reciprocal affection even if it is not obvious. The apparent lack of affection and lack of response to affection from others, including George and me, have been the hardest characteristic for me to live with. However, as Mary Ann has matured, it has slowly become clear that she does in fact offer affection and she certainly appreciates receiving it, even though she still has difficulty verbalizing it. She often says to me "I like you" in a way that sounds both defensive and affectionate at the same time.

5. Seize every opportunity to share in her delight. Mary Ann loves birthday parties, both her own and those of her friends. She loves to sing favorite songs, from the *Sesame Street* version of "Twelve Days of Christmas" to Handel's "Hallelujah Chorus." Best of all for me is to sit in the background during her voice lessons as she sings and learns with incomparable zest. These have been the happiest days of my life—her joy is contagious.

Robert Herrick's poetry, like most lyric poetry, does not give us guidance on how to live our lives. It does not tell a story. It does not really communicate any essential information. It merely shares with us the imagery and music of language. Thus, it may soothe our psyche or it may excite us with the sheer magic of language. In other words, it serves not as communication but as pleasure.

Mary Ann's language, both English and Spanish, is closer to lyric poetry than to the everyday use of language as communication. Similarly, her pleasure riding the carousel constitutes an uninhibited joy. Her enthusiastic singing is another example of uninhibited joy. However, she is willing to share this pleasure with others and she is eager to improve its quality, much like the lyric poets of the seventeenth century.

Mary Ann's Effect on My Life

My formal education, including a master's degree and course work toward a doctorate in English literature, prepared me for a career as a college English teacher. When George and I were married, it was understood that the husband's career came before the wife's, therefore I was not free to conduct a standard search for a job teaching English. However, I was lucky in being able to substitute for professors on sabbatical leave for three and a half years at the State University of New York at Brockport while George designed optical instruments, including the periscope for the Nautilus, the first nuclear submarine, at Bausch and Lomb.

While waiting to have children, I participated in the Rochester Independent Political Forum and Women Strike for Peace. In less than three years, I learned the basics of civic protest, especially in Washington, DC. We worked hard, and successfully, to end the atmospheric testing of nuclear weapons. Then we did all we could to prevent a nuclear conflagration during the Cuban missile crisis, meeting in the Russian Embassy as well as marching in front of the White House.

Mary Ann was born one month after the assassination of President John F. Kennedy. I have sometimes wondered if that horrendous shock during my pregnancy might have contributed to her disability.

George and I were thrilled with her arrival and I moved away from civic activity, devoting all my time and attention to my new daughter. Mary Ann was twenty-two months old when her little brother Fred arrived. We were beginning to have questions about Mary Ann's development, but within a few months George had an opportunity for an exciting new job in Connecticut and off we went.

As indicated in chapter one, we were living in Connecticut when

Mary Ann's autism was discovered and she was fully evaluated. For much of 1968, I was again drawn to political activity and worked in Eugene McCarthy's presidential campaign, bringing little Fred and sometimes Mary Ann also along wherever I went, including to the office I ran. I still was resisting contact with other parents of autistic children. Looking back, I think I was afraid of the bad news I would hear.

Mary Ann spent one year in an interesting preschool program in Rowayton, Connecticut, after her evaluation at Yale. She was totally integrated with a group of non-disabled young children in this program. The original teacher had worked at the League School in Brooklyn, one of the earliest schools for children with autism in the country. Unfortunately, this teacher became seriously ill in the middle of the school year and had to leave. For Mary Ann, the rest of the year was mostly frustration.

Then George changed jobs again and we found ourselves in Huntington, Long Island, New York. By this time, I had no choice but to find the local branch of the Autism Society because I needed knowledgeable help in locating worthwhile programs for Mary Ann. On Long Island, Carol and Dennis Hansen, Phyllis Gold, and other parents were a huge help to me. They had helped found the Autism Society of America and they were knowledgeable, committed leaders in this pioneering effort.

As I became active in the local chapter of the Autism Society, I quickly learned how supportive parents can be to each other. This group of parents could share the same worries, the same challenges, even the same jokes.

After three years on Long Island, we moved finally to Lexington, Massachusetts. Lexington turned out to be a perfectly fine school system for both children. This time, however, we made a crucial error in finding a house. As usually happens when a family is relocating to a new town, we looked at houses on the weekend. We settled on a lovely little house at the foot of a wooded hillside without realizing that on weekdays, at commuter time, our idyllic street served as a busy shortcut from a major highway, Route 2, over to the city of Waltham.

This traffic hazard really isolated both children, but Mary Ann especially. She could not safely walk anywhere alone or even with Fred. Eventually we did find another house closer to the center of

Lexington. This early, hard lesson contributed to my resolve to find semi-independent adult housing for Mary Ann close to the center of town. Lexington, like so many suburban towns, had next to no public transportation—later it did establish a local bus system, but even now the hours are limited.

As I indicated in chapter four, I quickly became involved in the development and enactment of Massachusetts' revolutionary special education law. I have often thought our family's experience living in three earlier geographical locations and trying with minimal success to find appropriate programs for Mary Ann contributed mightily to my appreciation of this emerging new law and the federal law that soon followed.

On Long Island, I had discovered the value of working with other parents of autistic children and now, in Massachusetts, I was privileged to experience the knowledge, inspiration, and fellowship of parents of children with all different disabilities, as well as many of the young people themselves. Within another two years, this network began to expand across the country.

Thus Mary Ann's disability brought to me the joy and honor of working with parents of children with special needs all across this country, beginning with Barbara Cutler and others in Massachusetts and extending from Carmen Selles in Puerto Rico, to Mildred Hill in Georgia, to Judith Raskin in New Hampshire, to Betsy Brittin, now in California, Barbara Buswell in Colorado, Patty McGill Smith in Nebraska, Ursula Markey in New Orleans, Santiago Garcia serving migrant workers in Florida, and hundreds more—all sharing the same commitment to improving the lives of all our children, no matter what the special need might be and no matter the ethnic or economic status of the families.

In addition, I have benefited from the inspiration of another hundred or so professionals, all of whom have moved way beyond the "she's just a parent" attitude. These include the late Pat Trohanis, University of North Carolina; Percy Bates, University of Michigan (and former Acting Assistant Secretary of the federal Office of Special Education and Rehabilitative Services); Ed Martin, first Assistant Secretary of OSERS; Harvey Liebergott, special assistant to Ed Martin, and his wife Jacqueline Liebergott, now president of Emerson College; Doug Biklen, now a dean at Syracuse University; Tom Hehir, former director of the federal Office of Special Education Programs and now professor at Harvard; Madeleine Will, former Assistant Secretary of OSERS; and at least a hundred more, starting in Boston and spreading from there to Martin Kaufman, former dean at the University of Oregon.

Along the way, Mary Ann and I have become friends with some unbelievable heroes and heroines: Rob Cutler, Fred Fay, Jessica Vohs, Rick and Dick Hoyt, Christine Curran, Jane Smith, Michael Anderson, Bob Sneirson, Judy Heumann, Mike Ward, and many, many more.

*Mary Ann in Lexington center near the statue
of the Captain of the Minute Men*

Mary Ann's house on Waltham Street in Lexington had served as home to four women for a little over ten years. In the middle of the winter, well after Christmas, an invitation arrived in the mail, addressed to all four women. This was an invitation to join the Belfry Hill Neighborhood Association and come to the next meeting, scheduled for a Sunday afternoon in one of the churches across from Lexington Battle Green.

The belfry is a wooden tower sitting at the top of a hill overlooking the Green. It houses a replica of the bell used, on April 19, 1775, to summon the Minute Men to the Battle of Lexington to fight the British soldiers who, Paul Revere had warned, were on the way. This battle, of course, started the American Revolution.

Mary Ann and her housemates also were participating in an important revolution. Not many years ago, homes like theirs would have been subject to "NIMBY," in other words, "Not in My Back Yard," and efforts to keep them out would have almost always succeeded. For these women actually to be *invited* to join the local neighborhood association truly was revolutionary—and how fitting to be welcomed to the Belfry Hill Neighborhood Association.

Finally, this revolutionary invitation indicated that the local community, "the village," was learning to take on the role of protector in a warm, welcoming, respectful way.

I am confident that soon towns across this nation and much of the world will open their arms to welcome people with disabilities as participating citizens, and that we will finally see the end of the false protection of the Fernald Schools and the Pennhursts.

PART II:

From Poetry To History

CHAPTER 15

Well Intentioned Protection

A hundred years before Mary Ann was born, her great-great-grandparents, George W. and Maria Fotzinger Ziegler, were among the leading citizens in Greencastle, Pennsylvania, a small town south of Chambersburg and southwest of Gettysburg. The Zieglers' oldest son, George F., took a year off from his studies at Amherst College to enlist in the Union Army. As the fighting crept northward, the Zieglers decided to send their only daughter, Maria, then fifteen, off to safety in a boarding school in New Jersey. While there, she developed a fatal case of pneumonia, a century before antibiotics. She died far from home and family, leaving her father, aunt, and brother to grieve inconsolably. (Maria's mother had died several years earlier and her aunt helped to care for the children.) Letters, pictures, and mementos indicate that this grief consumed the survivors, especially Maria's older brother George Frederick, for the rest of their lives.

Mary Ann has survived several such well-intentioned efforts by family members, schools, and society in general. The drive to protect our children from harm is so strong that it sometimes overrides our awareness of less obvious dangers, and short-term protective measures may take precedence over longer term ones. For instance, Mary Ann contracted chicken pox in her late thirties. Dr. Martin Santis, our physician at the time, asked me, "Was she in essentially segregated settings in her earlier years?" He suggested that because she was not in a regular school setting, she was probably not exposed to the usual childhood diseases at an early age when they are less threatening. Of course today, most of these once-common childhood diseases are completely prevented by vaccination. Dr. Santis' observation provided one reason why people with Down syndrome and other disabilities live much longer today than they formerly did.

Segregated special classes, and even separate schools, were originally developed primarily to "protect" children with disabilities. In fact, historians tell us that Samuel Gridley Howe, who in 1848 founded the first state school for mentally retarded children, eventually known as the Walter E. Fernald State School in Massachusetts, "was one of the kindly citizens of the time who viewed these children as worthy of charity and compassion"[31] The schools that Howe developed "were intended to resemble a family setting. The pupils were believed to be happier here than they had been in their previous condition … [and] what they learned would help them be able to earn a living doing farm and household chores when they returned to their original communities." (I gained a new appreciation for Howe's intentions when I learned that he was married to Julia Ward Howe, the famous abolitionist and pacifist.)

Howe could not foresee that his special schools would soon evolve into quasi-prisons any more than the Ziegler family in Greencastle could predict that the dear daughter whom they were protecting from the horrors of war would contract a deadly infection and succumb far from home and caring family.

For the next 125 years, more and more children with disabilities were plucked from families and placed in various residential facilities, which were usually not the happy family setting that Howe envisioned. Sadly, it took 125 years before substantial progress resumed for our children with disabilities.

Finally, during the last quarter of the twentieth century, rapid and revolutionary change began to occur, with amazing effectiveness in view of its rapidity. By no means do I mean to imply that we have reached the ultimate goal for our people with disabilities, but we have made substantial progress and, more importantly, we have persuaded our policy makers to help continue the journey.

My daughter, Mary Ann, is a living embodiment of the recent change—a revolution that made the job of parenting both easier and harder for my late husband George and me. By necessity, we kept learning new meanings for the term "protection." At one point, when Mary Ann was eight years old, some of our relatives offered to pay to

---

31   Pfeiffer, David. *Ragged Edge Online*, Jan./Feb. 2003.

send her away to residential school. No doubt they thought this service would benefit her and also her younger brother Fred, but George and I were shocked. We loved Mary Ann and we had no intention of splitting up our family in this way. When we said, as politely as possible, "No, thank you," the subject was dropped and never came up again.

Without knowing much about the Fernald School or any of the residential schools for people with disabilities, we did know that Mary Ann belonged in our family, along with us, her brother Fred, the dog, Angie, and the cat, Peanut Butter. Together, we would provide the necessary protection for her just as we would for Fred.

Howe's assumption that a "special life," away from the demands of ordinary family life, is sometimes best for children is a fascinating illusion. Over the years, I have learned that this kind of step is often especially attractive, even seductive, for people of wealth and that plenty of residential programs are only too happy to accept the child and the money. It has been very difficult to overcome this kind of "protective urge" as we have worked so hard in the last thirty-five years to integrate our people with disabilities into normalized community living. Sometimes it is easier to overcome evil or neglect than to overcome well-intentioned, but inappropriate, protection.

CHAPTER 16
Out of the Wilderness: Chapter 766

Until 1975, public schools were not welcoming places for most children with disabilities. For instance, nearly all children using wheelchairs were forced to attend special, separate schools simply because ordinary public schools were full of stairs and other physical barriers. Chapter 750, the Massachusetts law covering emotionally disturbed children, also emphasized placement in separate, private schools, funded by the state. (Unbeknownst to George and me, Mary Ann was actually on a waiting list for such a school at the time. No doubt she was immediately placed on this list in order to save costs for the Town of Lexington. It was still legal for the school administration to take such a step without even notifying us as parents.) To keep out children with mobility limitations or seizure disorders, public schools cited problems with liability insurance. Such excuses did not even pretend to involve a goal of "protection" for the children. For parents, getting *any* education for their children was the highest priority; integration into regular schools was a far-off dream hardly even articulated in 1970–71.

Around this time, my friend Betsy Anderson took her five-year-old son to the local, neighborhood public school in Cambridge, Massachusetts. Michael, who was born with spina bifida, walked with braces at that time, and later used a wheelchair. However, he had no other significant disabilities, no mental retardation or cognitive challenges. When Betsy took him to the neighborhood school to enroll him in kindergarten, the principal said, "Oh we cannot have him here. He's a vegetable." That school had three floors, many stairs, and no elevators or ramps. Luckily, a new principal arrived in time to accept Michael and he attended his neighborhood school through second grade. The teachers moved their first and then second grade classes down to the first floor to accommodate Michael. The third grade teacher, however, refused to move her class down to the first floor where Michael could enter and the Andersons had no legal recourse. The family enrolled Michael in a private, "regular" school, the Cambridge Friends School, where he participated fully, learned, and flourished.

Today such barriers in public schools are illegal. A few may still exist, of course, but they are illegal and school departments must make changes.

Noreen Curran, another friend living in the Boston at the time, had a daughter Christine with Down syndrome. Because she had Down syndrome, Christine could not have access to a tutor for her learning disabilities even though she needed exactly that kind of service in order to learn to read. Christine also now lives and works independently in Watertown, the town where she grew up.

Unlike most states, Massachusetts did not have state-run schools for deaf or blind children, but it did have three or four highly regarded private schools for these two groups of children. For obvious reasons of distance, most of these children boarded at their schools and thus were almost totally isolated from their families and neighbors.

Throughout the state, hundreds of children classified as emotionally disturbed were at home, on waiting lists, waiting for an opening and tuition money in order to attend a well-intentioned, but probably mediocre, private school. Children with various disabilities were on waiting lists for openings in segregated, special classes in public schools. Those still living in institutions received minimal or no education provided by the institutions where they lived and no service of any kind from the community where their families resided. There was no absolute right for any of these children, including Mary Ann, to have an appropriate education.

So many children in the city of Boston were at home for months and years waiting to enter school that the organization now known as Massachusetts Advocates for Children prepared and widely disseminated a report entitled "Children Out of School." This report provided strong ammunition for our lobbying efforts; it persuasively underlined the gross inequality of the state's treatment of children with disabilities, especially those labeled emotionally disturbed.

In 1969, the Office of Planning and Program Coordination, a division of the Massachusetts Department of Administration and

Finance, sponsored a comprehensive, statewide report on the children then out of the mainstream of public education. Known as the MACE (Massachusetts Advisory Council on Education) Report, the authors were Burton Blatt and Frank Garfunkel, two well-known academics and advocates for children with disabilities. Near the end of the process, Doris Frazier, director of the Office of Planning and Program Coordination, contracted with Lawrence Kotin, then a young lawyer working for the Massachusetts Law Reform Institute, to conduct a legal analysis to be added to the report.

After reviewing special education laws in a few other states and studying the hodgepodge of discriminatory laws in Massachusetts, Kotin presented three major recommendations that were eventually incorporated in the new law:

1. Eliminate the separate categories of disability and base special education on a single category, "child with special needs."
2. Insure that every child will have a local community responsible for his/her education, preferably the community where the child lives.
3. Strengthen the special education part of the state Department of Education.

Kotin further emphasized the importance of a neutral funding formula so that the law would offer no incentive for any particular kind of placement, and that schools would offer a continuum of programs, from mainstreaming through varying degrees of separation, ultimately to specialized residential schools when absolutely necessary.

Over the years, I have become steadily more committed to the idea of a non-categorical approach to special education, and more appreciative of the miracle accomplished in Massachusetts, in spite of recent backsliding. The word "individual" in the IEP (Individualized Education Plan) was truly a revolutionary concept. When I was taking college education courses in 1950, I was taught to allow for "individual differences." However, no one taught me how to identify those "differences" or how to teach to them. Furthermore, as I think back, I realize that the range of differences being alluded to did not really include cerebral palsy, mental retardation, autism, or even dyslexia.

[Note: I use the term "mental retardation" in its historic usage, although I am very aware and grateful that this inaccurate and demeaning term has recently been discarded.]

At the time the Massachusetts law was enacted, I missed some of the significance of the shift to local responsibility, probably because that change was already in progress when we moved to Lexington. Still, after our strange experience on Long Island, with Mary Ann having to travel many miles in two counties in order to attend school, I should have recognized this importance immediately. Now that Mary Ann is an adult, living in the town where she grew up, her interrelationship with her local community is becoming stronger and stronger and steadily more important. As with so many things, she is teaching me more and more about the true, deep meaning of "community," not just acceptance but also belonging and participating. What a debt we owe to Larry Kotin for his vision in identifying this fundamental need for change in our education system. Perhaps even Larry did not realize at the time how dramatic this shift would prove to be throughout the lifetimes of the children.

As recently as January 2006, an article in *Newsday* described the harmful use of "time-out" rooms in segregated special education schools throughout Long Island. From Wantaugh, in Nassau County, to the eastern reaches of Suffolk County, children as young as seven with autism and other behavior disorders are basically imprisoned in totally segregated schools, often far from home. A hundred and fifty years after the founding of the Fernald State School, these modern-day children are being denied the support of their natural communities and families. Rather than being taught and nurtured, a child hears "Code C, Room 107" on the intercom and then four adults usher him/her into a padded room the size of a closet. If these children were being taught in a local public school, even in a segregated class, they would rarely be put in that "time-out" room. The local principal and teachers would be aghast at such treatment—they do not want their schools operating like prisons.

Robert Crabtree, then staff director for the Legislature's Joint Committee on Education, picked up on Kotin's work and then added components to ensure due process and parents' rights. Crabtree had become familiar with recent cases in the federal courts. One was the 1971 consent decree in the PARC (Pennsylvania Association for

Retarded Children v. Commonwealth of Pennsylvania) case that began as an effort by parents to improve conditions in the state's institutions for retarded children and then shifted to establishing a constitutional right to public education. This shift originally occurred for reasons of legal strategy. Research told lead attorney, Tom Gilhool, and the other lawyers that the precedent of Brown v. Topeka Board of Education, ending *de jure* segregation in our public schools, would serve as the strongest legal foundation for improving the lives of children in institutions. Therefore, the parents and legal team moved from "right to treatment" to "right to education." The lawyers involved in PARC realized that being properly treated in a large institution, as Howe had envisioned, was really not meaningful protection. Rather, the children then termed "mentally retarded" would move to a new level of protection if they could receive an appropriate, meaningful education and eventually participate in their home communities.

The other, equally important, court case was the decision in Mills v. Washington, DC Board of Education, which established a right to education for all children with handicapping conditions.[32] In this decision, the court ruled that no matter how strained the District of Columbia's funds for education might be, it could not reduce services for "handicapped" (the term current at the time) children, or any other single group, in order to have more money for "non-handicapped" children.

Tom Gilhool, the lawyer in the PARC case, with input from lawyer Stanley Herr and lawyer/professor Gunnar Dybwad, concluded that it was not enough to require that retarded children be present in public school classrooms. These men realized that without clearly stated rights and protections, such children were likely to be placed in the back of the classroom and largely ignored. From this realization came the notions of parental decision-making and what we now call the IEP (Individualized Education Plan), plus legal guarantees for each child. Bob Crabtree

---

32   *Mills v. Board of Education of the District of Columbia,* 348 F. Supp 866 (D. DC 1972), was a civil action brought in the District of Columbia federal district court on behalf of seven school-age children who sought their right to a free public education, which was being denied by the DC School Board. The Board alleged that the children could not be educated in public schools due to their "exceptional" needs, including mental illness and mental retardation, and it refused to provide private educational services because of high costs. Therefore, the children remained at home without access to an education.

inserted these requirements, and several other components, into the bill that was filed in the Massachusetts Legislature in 1971.

In developing language for these fundamental changes in the education of children with disabilities, Gilhool, Herr, and Crabtree also had access to a recently completed, model special education bill developed by the Council for Exceptional Children. This effort had been initiated and funded by the federal Bureau of Education for the Handicapped.

Clearly Gilhool, Crabtree, and the others realized that the strongest drive to protect and nurture children with disabilities resided with the children's parents. The PARC consent decree in 1971 was the crucial turning point in the history of protection for our children with disabilities. No longer would an isolated residential institution be required in order to insure adequate protection for them. In fact, they would be better protected if they could live with their families and go to school in their home communities with their neighbors and siblings, and eventually work there too.

Because of these visionary leaders, Mary Ann, like millions of others, has been able to live and work semi-independently in her home community. The salesman at the shoe store in downtown Lexington quietly said to me, "We watch out for them." Mary Ann's case manager at the state Department of Developmental Services calls her a "townie." Thus, Mary Ann lives within the protective embrace of her own community.

I realize, of course, that we still have a long way to go to guarantee community acceptance of all our people with disabilities. Still, we have come a very long way in a relatively short time.

By 1971, Larry Kotin was working for Massachusetts governor Frank Sargent—he and Bob Crabtree worked together to frame the bill that became the Bartley-Daly Law, familiarly referred to as Chapter 766. This revolutionary Massachusetts law was enacted in July 1972 with an effective date of September 1974. This two-year interval allowed time for all stakeholders—teachers, school administrators, state education department personnel, teacher training programs, and parents—to prepare for implementation.

During this important two-year interval which was set aside for planning, two more visionary leaders came to Massachusetts. Gregory Anrig, who would later head the Educational Testing Service, became

Commissioner of Education, and Robert Audette became State Director of Special Education.[33] These two worked together to develop comprehensive implementing regulations and to plan and conduct in-service training for public school administrators and teachers. Nevertheless, at the last minute during the summer of 1974, local municipal groups approached Speaker Bartley to try to postpone the change even longer. An educator himself, Bartley refused to make the change and insisted that the schools move ahead as planned.

Because Mary Ann was in an adequate elementary school program and I knew there were many children with special needs receiving no services even in Lexington, I chose to wait a year before referring her for the formal evaluation and development of an educational plan. That first IEP meeting was a chilling experience. Foolishly, I went to the meeting alone; without George and with no advocate or support person. The school psychologist was new and had recently met Mary Ann for the first time. He had nothing but negative things to say about her, nothing about the amazing progress she had made. His comments so devastated me that I could not participate effectively in the planning meeting. Never again did I attend one of these meetings alone; either George or a parent advocate came with me.

Food Note: Once I became fully engaged with legislative activity, and then working full-time, our family began to eat in restaurants regularly. Mary Ann quickly developed a taste for Chinese food, then Greek, and finally Mexican. Not long after we moved to Lexington, a new Chinese restaurant, Yangtze River, opened in the center of town. The owners and staff soon became extended family for us. Even today, thirty years later, Mary Ann is warmly welcomed there, often going in alone. She mastered chopsticks before any of the rest of the family did and she *loves* a Chinese buffet, mainly I think, because she can repeatedly fill her plate with meat and chicken and just a suggestion of vegetables. In spite of her autistic language limitations, Mary Ann has become so adept at ordering from a restaurant menu that waiters often seem unaware of her disability.

---

33   Robert Audette is now a professor in the education department at the University of North Carolina, Charlotte. Gregory Anrig is deceased.

CHAPTER 17

"Zero Reject." Lessons Learned from Legislative Success

The drafting and enactment of Chapter 766 holds many lessons for education advocacy efforts. I have already mentioned the importance of building an early coalition of stakeholders. It was especially important for the leaders of this effort to identify the common, shared issues of everyone involved: the various disability organizations, especially parent leaders; leading, knowledgeable educators; leaders in pediatric medicine and the various therapeutic professions; and leaders of other civic organizations like the League of Women Voters and the Greater Boston Chamber of Commerce. Getting input from all these varying groups from the beginning played a strategic role in building a strong, ultimately united, lobbying force that was difficult for any legislator to resist.

This group of citizen organizations, adopting the name Coalition for Special Education, met at least once a month throughout the year or so of active lobbying. I soon became co-chair of the Coalition, along with Betty Joel from the state chapter of the National Association of Social Workers (NASW). After the law was enacted in July 1972, the Coalition continued to play an active role in developing the implementing regulations and helping prepare parents and professionals for the new roles we would be playing.

Timing was also crucial for achieving this comprehensive change. Significant action was occurring in the federal courts that also strengthened our legislative work, such as the consent decree in the PARC (Pennsylvania Association for Retarded Children) case, followed by Mills. In the paragraph above, I mentioned two important reports issued in Massachusetts and, in addition, the state's League of Women Voters had spent a year or more studying the education of children with disabilities and its findings contributed to the law and to the lobbying effort. Although I did not realize it at the time, Ed Martin, then head of the federal Bureau of Education for the Handicapped, along with other federal leaders, including Senators and Congressmen, were already thinking about major changes in the federal special education laws.

The Bureau of Education for the Handicapped (BEH), a part of the federal Office of Education, sponsored and funded a public service program called Closer Look, a nationwide public awareness campaign. The campaign had been operating for a year or two before efforts were begun to change state and local laws. Led by Harvey Liebergott, at BEH, and James Green, vice president of Grey North Advertising in Chicago, the campaign used the services of several professionals in acting and advertising to saturate print, radio, and television media with public service announcements that very effectively promoted the importance of equal opportunity for people with disabilities, starting with education. By impacting the attitudes of parents, teachers, and the general public, this campaign laid the groundwork for the new laws that were about to become effective. The Closer Look campaign helped to create a crucial readiness for change among the key stakeholders. This visionary federal campaign also began to change the awareness of people in general, helping to prepare the public for integration of people with disabilities and thus advancing community protection.

Another concurrent development going on in the background was the growing national consumer movement. People were beginning to feel empowered as knowledgeable, even demanding consumers of safe automobiles, food, and other commodities. The new stage being set by Ralph Nader and other leaders of the consumer movement was creating psychological change that was carrying over into many arenas, including education.

As Larry Kotin observed and others agreed, "This was a time of civil rights, civil disobedience, and public activism." A few years earlier, I had myself been active in the movement to end atmospheric testing of atomic weapons and several of my friends had been active in the civil rights movement and the efforts to end the war in Vietnam. In other words, our generation's awakening to the possibilities of active citizenship had given us the courage and drive needed to bring about change on behalf of our children with disabilities. Furthermore, many of our legislators had themselves participated in these areas of citizen activism before they entered politics, and thus they were receptive to what they were hearing.

As I indicated above, before having children I had a personal history of political activism. In Rochester, I had been active in Women Strike for Peace. Later, in Connecticut, I worked in the presidential campaign of Eugene McCarthy.

Another factor, often overlooked, was the rapid progress within special education itself. Teacher educators at the University of Oregon, Syracuse University, University of Minnesota, Vanderbilt University, and other colleges and universities were developing new teaching methods and practices that established, once and for all, the fact that *all* children could learn, no matter how disabled they might be by language, sensory, or cognitive disabilities. In other words, no children need be discarded as hopeless. These ideas, too, were revolutionary.

Looking back, I think a major reason why I became so active in this legislative effort, assuming leadership at various points, was the experience our family had had in two other, reputedly progressive states before arriving in Massachusetts. And, of course, the blatant discrimination against my daughter contributed mightily to my motivation as it did to the motivation of my friends in the Coalition for Special Education.

Massachusetts' Chapter 766 had been implemented for only one year when the similar federal special education law was enacted, with an immediate effective date. President Gerald Ford signed the Education of All Handicapped Children Act into law in November 1975.

In the years immediately following the enactment of the federal law, the Bureau of Education for the Handicapped funded a large national program, referred to as the Deans' Grants, that helped large and small colleges and universities change their teacher training programs in order to comply with the new federal law. I had the privilege of working with Maynard Reynolds, then professor of education at the University of Minnesota, and several deans of education on an advisory committee. Through that experience, I discovered some of the rich new ways of thinking and planning that were already underway in teacher education. I will always remember a workshop I conducted at the College of St. Rose in Albany, New York, where a professor in the business department commented, "Well, teaching students as individuals, with individual needs, is nothing new to us—we have been forced to do that for a long time."

Dean Corrigan, then dean of education at Texas A&M, taught me the phrase "zero reject"—in other words, starting in November of 1975, no child or group of children could any longer be excluded from a public education. It had only taken two hundred years to reach that point! Much later I learned how checkered the whole history of compulsory education had been, with a few states not requiring education until well into the twentieth century. Even now we sometimes see more emphasis on protecting and nurturing livestock, corn, and other grains headed for market than on protecting and educating our children.

Finally, passage of the Massachusetts law and the federal law three years later was a major tribute to democracy at its best—knowledgeable legislators and staff, parents, educators and other professionals, and leaders of civic organizations all uniting to improve the lives of vulnerable children by spelling out and insuring the civil rights of these children and their parents. This working combination of committed, knowledgeable adults from a variety of professions had come together to develop a whole new paradigm of protection for our vulnerable children. As I said earlier, from the beginning of the legislative process, this effort received bipartisan support. Then, as now, the Massachusetts Legislature was overwhelmingly Democratic, but the governor, Frank Sargent, was Republican, and after passage by the Legislature, he happily signed the bill into law. Likewise, three years later, it was Democratic senators and congressmen who took the lead, albeit with the support of their Republican colleagues, and a Republican president, Gerald Ford, who signed the bill into federal law.

As the enactment date drew near in Massachusetts, more and more worries surfaced about how the new law would be funded. Key staff members in the office of the state's Secretary of Education responded to this challenge and developed in-depth cost estimates as best they could. Many of the components of the law were so new, and the mandate so universal, that it was very difficult to produce accurate numbers, but the estimates were realistic enough that they succeeded in quelling the objections.

As I reflect on that year or so of advocacy and lobbying, I am amazed to recall how meager the opposition was—in Massachusetts, opponents were largely limited to a few private special education schools whose leaders felt threatened. Those of us leading the lobbying effort managed to reach several compromises that satisfied the opposition without sacrificing the rights of the children and parents. For instance, children then in private school were grandfathered in their placement while some of us silently hoped that most of these parents would discover how much better their children's education could be now in public school.

The state law and the federal law that followed it had several important side effects. The first was the strengthening of families. As parents, especially mothers, acquired new knowledge and skills in implementing our children's rights, our own self-esteem as parents grew and we learned to approach our children's teachers and doctors as colleagues, as equals on behalf of our children, and as teammates committed to the protection and nurture of our children.

Yulika Forman, who recently received her doctorate in education at Tufts University, shared with me some of her experience in conducting a study of families of children with disabilities in Russia and the Ukraine. She found that as they gained significant knowledge about their children's disability, they also gained self-esteem and confidence as parents. This too constitutes a revolutionary change for parents of children with disabilities, especially autism, after decades of being outright blamed for their children's disability.

A second, profound change was the coming together of all the various individual disability organizations and our discovery that we had more shared interests than differences. That change, too, has continued. No doubt, this crucial movement was facilitated by the law's emphasis on "*child* with special needs." How can reasonable people say "My child is more deserving than your child?" This union of disability organizations was crucial, not only to enact and implement the federal special education law, but also to enact and enforce the Americans with Disabilities Act fifteen years later.

A third, less obvious, positive change has been progress toward the equalization across racial, ethnic, and socioeconomic lines for everyone involved with the education of children with disabilities, especially parents. Like so much social progress in this country, change in special education began primarily, although not exclusively, with middle-class white families through the work of mothers who had the time and resources needed to conduct extensive, in-depth volunteer work. However, in short order, the early leaders realized that large numbers of minority children and families were not actively represented in the work and that these families should also be heard, and that they too had major contributions to make.

As I indicated above, the Coalition for Special Education continued to meet for several years, first helping to develop the implementing regulations and then gearing up for passage of the federal special education law, originally called the Education of All Handicapped Children Act, and usually referred to as P.L. 94—142, later renamed IDEA (Individuals with Disabilities Education Act.) One of the many, truly remarkable aspects of this federal law is the fact that Part B of the law, the section much like the Massachusetts law that sets forth the process for individual children, was enacted "in perpetuity." In other words, that basic section of the law never needs to be reauthorized, unlike nearly all other federal laws. Of course, it can be amended, and it has been several times.

Several of us who were active parents in Massachusetts kept talking to each other, and in 1974, we decided to recruit representatives from the major parent-run disability organizations in order to establish the Federation for Children with Special Needs. We deliberately chose the phrase "children with special needs" in order to reinforce the new emphasis on individual children instead of the old categorical labels. Once the new law was in place, we realized that parents needed to acquire a whole new set of skills and knowledge—the days of selling cookies and Christmas cards in order to support a desperate, little private program were over (or should be over).

David Trott, a young graduate of Harvard Law School, was awarded an American Council on Education fellowship which enabled him to work full-time for the Federation, helping us complete the legal requirements for incorporation and tax exempt status and to think through the details of formal organization. He also wrote a legal newsletter called *Focus* for us to distribute to parents, informing them of their and their children's rights under the new law. I was chosen as executive director of the new Federation. The other leading founders included Betsy Anderson, Spina Bifida Association; Beverly Graham, Association for Mentally Retarded Children; Pat Theroux, Association for Children with Learning Disabilities; Roy Cummings, parents of deaf children; and Joan Schaub, parents of blind children.

Together, we founding parents decided it was now time for parents to be paid for our hard-won knowledge and expertise, and for sharing that knowledge in an organized, structured way. At this time, Harvey Liebergott, who worked in the Boston Regional Office of the federal Bureau of Education for the Handicapped (BEH) and was the inspiration behind the Closer Look campaign, persuaded his boss, Ed Martin, director of BEH and later first assistant secretary of the Office of Special Education and Rehabilitative Services (OSERS), to experiment with federal funding for organizations of parents who would help other parents implement the new federal program about to be signed into law.

BEH funded a pilot project with the Federation to see how such an idea would work. Of course, we were immediately swamped with requests from parents seeking information and guidance. Before the end of our eighteen-month contract, BEH issued a Request for Proposals (RFP) designed to fund five Parent Information Centers (PICs) in the country for a period of three years. The original five PICs that won this initial competition were located in Boston, Massachusetts; Chicago, Illinois; Cincinnati, Ohio; Concord, New Hampshire, and South Bend, Indiana. We published regular newsletters, conducted information meetings throughout our states, and responded to an unbelievable number of telephone inquiries.

While we were getting the Federation off the ground, parents and other advocates across the country were working hard to frame and enact the federal special education mandate—the Education of All Handicapped Children Act (later renamed the Individuals with Disabilities Education Act or IDEA), which was signed into law in November 1975. A crucially important federal law that guarantees an appropriate public education for all children with disabilities, IDEA has since been amended several times, usually by addition of new programs or strengthening existing components, and occasionally by harmful tinkering.

The Federation had been operating for less than a year when we succeeded in landing a grant from our state's Developmental Disabilities Planning Council to train "lay advocates"—non-lawyers who could represent parents in due process hearings. The training was conducted by teams of lawyers and parents. This training, which took place in three parts of the state, helped fill a great need, but it also created even more demand for the Federation's services. Before long, questions arose about the legality of having non-lawyers represent parents in formal due process hearings. After careful research and discussion, Ed Martin issued a formal policy statement declaring that this practice is, indeed, legal.[34]

The PIC program had been a temporary, innovative program with no guaranteed future. With guidance from Tom Behrens, who served in the Division of Personnel Preparation (DPP) at BEH, the PICs gradually shifted over to funding from the three-year grant competitions under DPP. This shift was very complicated because, at the time, the states were divided into three groups, with one group eligible for grants each year. Thus, some of the PICs, including the Federation, would have been stranded with no money had it not been for creative thinking by Tom Behrens and his boss, Jasper Harvey.

Luckily, the total budget for DPP kept increasing slowly but steadily, and thus the Division could gradually include more and more parent centers, now called Parent Training and Information (PTI) projects in order to fit credibly within Personnel Preparation. At the time, DPP was the most logical place for the parent centers among the relatively small number of grant programs within the Office of Special Education Programs. Also, it was the program with the largest amount of flexible funding.

In 1983, we succeeded in adding to the federal law a separate section establishing Parent Training and Information centers. At one point, Betsy Britten, then director of the Cincinnati parent center, and I sat at a typewriter in the office of Senator Lowell Weicker, then Chairman of the Subcommittee dealing with special education. Betsy and I together literally composed most of the statutory language for the Parent Centers.

Others added a section that established a national technical assistance program for the parent centers. The Federation won the first competition and the resulting program was known as TAPP (Technical Assistance for Parent Programs). The number of PTI programs grew rapidly from seventeen at the time of inclusion in the law, to forty at

---

34   In November of 2007, Ed Martin was elected to a three-year term as mayor of Venice, Florida.

the start of the TAPP Project, to over seventy in 2000, and eventually to more than one hundred.

Then, in 1986, a whole new program for serving very young children, birth to age three, was added to the federal law—now called IDEA. This Early Intervention program allowed each state to select a lead agency rather than rely solely on a state's Department of Education. Massachusetts, for instance, chose the Department of Public Health. Originally known as Part H, this program further strengthened the role of parents and families. It actually called for an IFSP, an Individual Family Service Plan rather than an IEP (Individual Education Plan), the requirement in IDEA. The new Early Intervention program reinforced the role of families as equal, significant players in the education and care of young children with disabilities.

Ironically, these new Early Intervention programs, serving children from birth to age three, have barely begun to help children with autism simply because the average age of diagnosis is still so late—twenty-four to thirty or thirty-six months. Thus, most autistic children receive only about a year of early intervention, and much of that time is taken up with evaluation and planning.

In the 1990 reauthorization of IDEA, a program of Experimental Projects or Community Parent Resource Centers (CPRCs) was added to the law. The CPRCs were the brainchild of Congressman Major Owens, of Brooklyn, New York.[35] He recognized how hard it was for inner- city minority parents and those living in isolated rural areas to access the services of the PTIs. At the Federation, we had tried very hard to be inclusive, but it was difficult to overcome barriers of race, ethnicity, and socioeconomic status. An amendment to the Federation's national technical assistance grant allowed us to fund five centers as CPRC models and then gradually to add to the list.

I was struggling to figure out where to begin to implement this new initiative when Charlotte "Dee" Spinkston came along from nowhere to apply for the new position as director of the effort. Dee had read about the initiative and the job in the Federation's newsletter. She was immediately off and running, quickly identifying five solid groups around the country to start this new program. Dee was perfect for

---

35   Major Owens retired from Congress at the end of his term in January 2007. He
      was a strong supporter of people with disabilities and played a significant role
      in enacting the Americans with Disabilities Act.

this new role. She is African American, the sister of a brother with a disability, and a professional in deaf/blind education. Dee is fluent in three different interpreting languages.

These community-based parent centers now number twenty-five. Several of their leaders have become the most effective parent leaders in the country.

I consider the development of the CPRCs the most important success of the TAPP Project. Among the leaders who quickly emerged are "Sweet Alice" Harris of Watts in Los Angeles, Ursula Markey of New Orleans, and Santiago Garcia, who represents migrant worker families in Homestead, Florida. Two other remarkable centers are the Vietnamese Parents of Disabled Children in Los Angeles, and a group in the Pine Ridge Lakota Reservation in South Dakota. We soon discovered that these spectacular heroes, among others, had as much to teach the rest of us as they had to learn from us. While most of the PTI leaders warmly welcomed these newcomers, a few still lived with old prejudices, and a few others still saw no need for this kind of separateness and felt they could successfully include everyone within their existing organization. Sometimes this form of denial is harder to overcome than out-and-out segregation or prejudice.

The CPRC program demonstrates the importance of federal funding, even insufficient funding, because these parent leaders could not possibly afford to perform their necessary work for our nation's neediest families without this kind of financial stability. Including them in the larger network has enriched the work of all of us.

Almost immediately, leaders of the CPRCs banded together to form The Grassroots Consortium in order to help each other and to learn and grow together. Agnes Johnson, of SKI (Special Kids, Inc.) in Houston, was chosen to head Grassroots, and Ursula Markey volunteered to publish a regular newsletter called *Tapestry*.

As executive director of the Federation and head of the TAPP Project for several years, I was able to work closely with an amazing variety of families throughout the nation and a few in other countries. All of them inspired me with their commitment, their sense of humor, their knowledge, and their eagerness to go on learning indefinitely. Mary Ann also benefited greatly from many of these people; the late Carmen Selles de Vila, founder of the PTI in Puerto Rico, and

Charlotte DesJardins, founder of the Chicago PTI, are virtual family members for Mary Ann.

Food Note: In the early years of the growing PTI network, we often held national conferences at an inexpensive, church-operated meeting resort on Cape Cod. Sometimes I took Mary Ann along. One time when we went to the dining area for supper, Mary Ann was shocked to discover there was no meat. She complained loudly and bitterly. Meanwhile, my friend Mildred Hill, from the Georgia PTI, struggled to conceal her laughter—she agreed with Mary Ann.

Later in the evening, Paula Goldberg, director of the parent center in Minneapolis and the contingent from Minnesota, arrived at the door of the meeting room. Mary Ann answered the door and said insistently, "Where's the meat?" Shortly afterward, Paula and the rest of the Minnesota group went shopping for cold cuts for Mary Ann.

CHAPTER 18

Variety in Parent Advocacy

One night, Lani Guinier was being interviewed by Emily Rooney on Boston's public TV program, *Greater Boston*. Emily asked Lani about her reaction when President Clinton retracted her nomination for a high position in the Justice Department. Guinier responded that she had benefited greatly from advice that she had received from Roger Wilkinson. Wilkinson had told her that Americans do not like a victim and, therefore, she should adopt a cause.

Even though we were not consciously thinking along these lines that is exactly what parents of children with disabilities were doing in the early 1970s—setting aside the notion of our children and ourselves as "victims" and adopting the cause of equal rights, beginning with education. Once you adopt a cause, you cannot give up until you succeed. In fact, you keep on converting more and more people to join your cause if it is a just one.

The death of my good friend, Chuck Harrison, reminded me once again of the variety of kinds of advocacy by parents. Chuck helped start several programs, including a day school, a respite program, and the Massachusetts chapter of Autism Society of America. He also served on key governmental advisory committees, in addition to several boards of directors, for many years. His advocacy occurred in the background, not in the limelight, but it was effective and necessary nonetheless. Chuck performed roles that helped others accomplish the more obvious advocacy and lobbying roles.

At the same time, another approach was growing in other parts of the country. Parent-to-Parent started simultaneously in Nebraska and California, with Mary Slaughter, Shirley Dean, Florene Poyadue, and Patty Smith playing leading roles. Instead of working directly to change laws, this approach worked to strengthen and empower parents as parents. Like Chuck Harrison's work, Parent-to-Parent also occurred more in the background, with one parent helping another parent in a variety of ways. Eventually, by 1975, all the varying approaches, including our active lobbying efforts in Massachusetts, combined to create revolutionary change in the lives of children with disabilities and their families.

Both Parent-to-Parent and the active lobbying efforts relied, to some extent, on the work of older, separate disability organizations also usually founded by parents. However, with the growth of Parent-to-Parent and the Parent Training and Information (PTI) centers, parents came together across disabilities, for the first time becoming a generic disability movement. Over the years, these two major parallel groups intersected and occasionally merged at a local level. As one might expect, sometimes competition and mistrust developed. Local Parent-to-Parent groups sometimes mistrusted their PTI neighbors because the PTI received federal government money. In fact, willingness to receive government funding created a split among the original parent coalitions, with one in central California unwilling even to compete for the grants.

The federal government has played a key role in the growth and health of both parent movements—the US Department of Education and eventually Congress in the case of PTIs, and the Department of Maternal and Child Health (HHS) in the case of Parent-to-Parent.

It is important to note that meaningful, informed involvement by parents has become a more and more significant part of education laws, particularly special education laws.

Almost simultaneously, adults with disabilities were also organizing on their own, becoming eloquent, effective self-advocates, first in the Independent Living movement and later joining with parents in the movement to enact the Americans with Disabilities Act.

Some of the early pioneers who chose to keep their children with disabilities at home and in the neighborhood school endured considerable suffering. I remember the anguish of a mother speaking at an early hearing about the federal law, probably in 1972 or so. Living in a small town in far, northern New Hampshire, near the Canadian border, she talked about the attacks she and her family experienced because they had a child with an obvious disability—ongoing verbal criticism and even physical attacks on their car and house. There was no obvious recourse for this family—no Sec. 504, much less ADA, no federal special education law to be enforced by the federal government, and no legal rights at all for the child or the family.

My life with disability has been all about autism. However, because of my nearly forty years of work in disability advocacy and policy, I have expanded that experience to incorporate the large, varied arena of disabilities. Furthermore, Mary Ann and I both have learned much from our many friends with disabilities other than autism.

PART III:

Appendices

Appendix A
Hallmark Developmental Milestones

(Permission granted by Nancy Wiseman,
First Signs, Inc. All rights reserved.)

Does Your Baby...

At Four Months:
- Follow and react to bright colors, movement, and objects?
- Turn toward sounds?
- Show interest in watching people's faces?
- Smile back when you smile?

At Six Months:
- Relate to you with real joy?
- Smile often while playing with you?
- Coo or babble when happy?
- Cry when unhappy?

At Nine Months:
- Smile and laugh while looking at you?
- Exchange back-and-forth smiles, loving faces, and other expressions with you?
- Exchange back-and-forth sounds with you?
- Exchange back-and-forth gestures with you, such as giving, taking, and reaching?

At Twelve Months:
- Use a few gestures, one after another, to get needs met, like giving, showing, reaching, waving, and pointing?
- Play peek-a-boo, patty cake, or other social games?
- Make sounds, like "ma," "ba," "na," "da," and "ga?"
- Turn to the person speaking when his/her name is called?

At Fifteen Months:
- Exchange with you many back-and-forth smiles, sounds, and gestures in a row?
- Use pointing or other "showing" gestures to draw attention to something of interest?
- Use different sounds to get needs met and draw attention to something of interest?
- Use and understand at least three words, such as "mama," "dada," "bottle," or "bye-bye"?

At Eighteen Months:
- Use lots of gestures with words to get needs met, like pointing or taking you by the hand and saying, "want juice"?
- Use at least four different consonants in babbling or words, such as m, n, p, b, t, and d?
- Use and understand at least ten words?
- Show that he or she knows the names of familiar people or body parts by pointing to or looking at them when they are named?
- Do simple pretend play, like feeding a doll or stuffed animal, and attracting your attention by looking up at you?

At Twenty-Four Months:
- Do pretend play with you with more than one action, like feeding the doll and then putting the doll to sleep?
- Use and understand at least fifty words?
- Use at least two words together, without imitating or repeating, in a way that makes sense, like "want juice"?

- Enjoy being next to children of the same age and show interest in playing with them? Perhaps giving a toy to another child?
- Look for familiar objects out of sight when asked?

At Thirty-Six Months:
- Enjoy pretending to play different characters with you or talking for dolls or action figures?
- Enjoy playing with children of the same age? Perhaps showing and telling another child about a favorite toy?
- Use thoughts and actions together in speech and in play in a way that makes sense, like "sleepy, go take nap" and "baby hungry, feed bottle"?
- Answer "what," "where," and "who" questions easily?
- Talk about interests and feelings about the past and the future?

The key social, emotional, and communication milestones were compiled from the following sources: Greenspan, S.I. (1999) *Building Healthy Minds*, Perseus Books; Prizant, B.M., Wetherby, A.M., Roberts, J.E. (2000) *Communication Disorders in Infants and Toddlers*, In C. Zeanah (Ed.) *Handbook of Infant Mental Health, Second Edition*, New York: Guilford Press; and Wetherby, A.M. (1999) *Babies Learn to Talk at an Amazing Rate*, FIRST WORDS Project, Florida State University.

The author wishes to thank the following people who contributed to these milestones: Ilene Beal; Frances P. Glascoe, PhD.; Rebecca Landa, PhD.; and Robert H. Wharton, MD.

APPENDIX B
Autism Organizations

**National Institute of Neurological Disorders and Stroke
National Institutes of Health**

**Association for Science in Autism
Treatment**
P.O. Box 188
Crosswicks, NJ 08515-0188
info@asatonline.org
http://www.asatonline.org

**Autism Network International
(ANI)**
P.O. Box 35448
Syracuse, NY 13235-5448
jisincla@syr.edu
http://www.ani.ac

Autism Society of America
7910 Woodmont Ave.
Suite 300
Bethesda, MD 20814-3067
http://www.autism-society.org
Tel: 301-657-0881 / 800-3AUTISM
(328-8476)
Fax: 301-657-0869

**Birth Defect Research for
Children, Inc.**
800 Celebration Avenue, Suite 225
Celebration, FL 34747
betty@birthdefects.org
http://www.birthdefects.org
Tel: 407-566-8304 / Fax: 407-566-8341

**Autism National Committee
(AUTCOM)**
P.O. Box 429
Forest Knolls, CA 94933
http://www.autcom.org

Autism Research Institute (ARI)
4182 Adams Avenue
San Diego, CA 92116
director@autism.com
http://www.autismresearchinstitute.com
Tel: 619-281-7165 / Fax: 619-563-6840

Autism Speaks, Inc.
2 Park Avenue, 11th Floor
New York, NY 10016
contactus@autismspeaks.org
http://www.autismspeaks.org
Tel: 212-252-8584 / California: 310-230-3568
Fax: 212-252-8676

**MAAP Services for Autism, Asperger
Syndrome, and PDD**
P.O. Box 524
Crown Point, IN 46308
info@maapservices.org
http://www.maapservices.org
Tel: 219-662-1311 / Fax: 219-662-0638

National Dissemination Center for Children with Disabilities
U.S. Dept. of Education, Office of Special Education Programs
P.O. Box 1492
Washington, DC 20013-1492
nichcy@aed.org
http://www.nichcy.org
Tel: 800-695-0285 / Fax: 202-884-8441

National Institute on Deafness and Other Communication Disorders Information Clearinghouse
1 Communication Avenue
Bethesda, MD 20892-3456
nidcdinfo@nidcd.nih.gov
http://www.nidcd.nih.gov
Tel: 800-241-1044 800-241-1055 (TTD/TTY)

National Institute of Mental Health (NIMH)
National Institutes of Health, DHHS
6001 Executive Blvd. Rm. 8184,
MSC 9663
Bethesda, MD 20892-9663
nimhinfo@nih.gov
http://www.nimh.nih.gov
Tel: 301-443-4513/866-415-8051 /
301-443-8431 (TTY)
Fax: 301-443-4279

National Institute of Child Health and Human Development (NICHD)
National Institutes of Health, DHHS
31 Center Drive, Rm. 2A32 MSC 2425
Bethesda, MD 20892-2425
http://www.nichd.nih.gov
Tel: 301-496-5133 / Fax: 301-496-7101

National Institute of Environmental Health Sciences (NIEHS)
National Institutes of Health, DHHS
111 T.W. Alexander Drive
Research Triangle Park, NC 27709
webcenter@niehs.nih.gov
http://www.niehs.nih.gov
Tel: 919-541-3345

Note: For regular, latest information, I recommend the Schafer Autism Report, available by email at www.sarnet.org.

Self-Advocacy: For comprehensive national and international information about the exciting self-advocacy movement, go to the Autistic Self Advocacy Network at www.autisticselfadvocacy.org. Leading autistic self-advocates include Temple Grandin, Stephen Shore, William Stillman, and Ari Ne'eman, among others.

APPENDIX C

Parent Training and Information (PTI) Programs and Community Parent Resource Centers (CPRCs)

To locate a federally funded parent center, go to the following Web page:

PACER Center, www.pacer.org.

or

Phone
(8:00 AM to 5:00 PM CST, Monday through Friday)
Minnesota: 800-537-2237 or 952-838-9000
TTY: 952-838-0190
USA: 888-248-0822
Fax: 952-838-0199

Mailing Address
PACER Center, Inc.
8161 Normandale Blvd.
Bloomington, MN 55437

You can also contact the Federation for Children with Special Needs, http://fcsn.org.

Federation for Children with Special Needs
1135 Tremont Street, Suite 420
Boston, MA 02120
Phone: 617-236-7210, 800-331-0688 (in MA)
Fax: 617-572-2094
Email: fcsninfo@fcsn.org

Manufactured By: RR Donnelley
                     Momence, IL USA
                     May, 2010